Favorite BIBLE HEROES

For Ages 4 & 5

Publisher .... *Arthur L. Miley*
Author .... *Nancy Sanders*
Managing Editor .... *Jack Cavanaugh*
Editorial Director .... *Carol Rogers*
Art Director .... *Deborah Birch*
Cover Design .... *Court Patton*
Production Coordinator .... *Chris D. Neynaber*
Illustrators .... *Jo Ann Hall*
Terry J. Walderhaug
Proofreader .... *Heather Swindle*

Rainbow Books

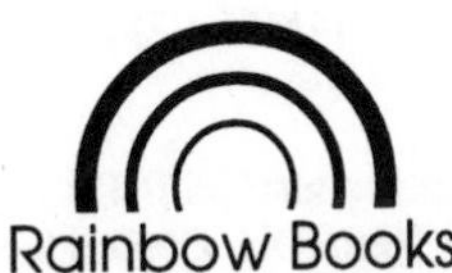

Rainbow Books • P.O. Box 261129 • San Diego, CA 92196

#RB36197
ISBN 0-937282-23-5

This book is dedicated to Virginia and Larry Sanders.
Through their acceptance and love, my life has been made complete.
I love each of them for who they are
and am grateful that God has allowed me to be a part of their lives.

Nancy I. Sanders

Unless otherwise indicated, all Scripture is taken from
the KING JAMES VERSION of the Bible.

Introduction

Young children are eager to play and experience the world around them. The crafts, puzzles, games, and activities in *Favorite Bible Heroes for Ages 4 & 5,* creatively channel this energy into positive Bible learning experiences. As the children learn about the struggles and adventures of 13 Old and New Testament Bible Heroes, they begin to apply the biblical concepts to their own lives.

Each Bible activity contains the following:

- **BIBLE HERO** name and/or picture
- **LESSON TITLE** highlighting a particular event or Bible story
- **SCRIPTURE REFERENCE** for further reading and/or background information
- **MEMORY VERSE** to reinforce the story or lesson
- **INTRODUCTION** of the Bible hero and his or her story
- **FOR THE TEACHER** directions, materials needed, and pre-class preparation
- **ACTIVITY TITLE & PROJECT DESCRIPTION** which may be read directly to the children.

HINTS are interspersed throughout the book and include helpful ideas for expanding the project, making it more cost effective, or adapting it to meet the special needs of young learners and pre-readers. Discussion starters encourage the children to apply the biblical concepts to their own lives. Suggestions for directed conversation appear in bold type. Inexpensive school supplies and household materials help keep craft expenses to a minimum. A reproducible NOTE TO FAMILIES, requesting their help in acquiring supplies, appears on page 7.

Safety should be a priority. Do not let children handle staplers or other sharp objects. Close supervision is recommended at all times.

These crafts and activities highlight various aspects of just a few of the diverse people whose stories are portrayed in the pages of the Bible. The common thread that runs through each of their lives is the transforming power of knowing God personally. Through this relationship with God, their ordinary lives are joined together in an extraordinary purpose: to share the hope that is found through Christ Jesus. Use the activities in *Favorite Bible Heroes for Ages 4 & 5* to enable young children to discover the hope found in Christ Jesus for themselves.

TABLE OF CONTENTS

MEMORY VERSE INDEX

Old Testament

New Testament

REPRODUCIBLE NOTE TO FAMILIES

For your convenience, the following page contains notes to families, requesting their help in collecting the materials necessary to complete the craft activities. Hand out these notes two or three weeks before you need the items. Specify whether items should be brought in at any time or only on a specific date. Then simply duplicate the notes, and send one home with each child.

To Families of Four- and Five-Year-Olds

We have some exciting activities planned for use in teaching Bible lessons this year. Some of these crafts and projects utilize household items. We'd like to ask your help in saving these items for our activities. Here is a list of some of the items that we are collecting:

- ☐ adhesive-backed magnetic strips
- ☐ small adhesive bandages
- ☐ aluminum foil
- ☐ blue tissue paper
- ☐ 12 x 17-inch boxes or larger
- ☐ burger boxes from fast-food restaurants
- ☐ flat buttons
- ☐ taper candles
- ☐ large candy canes, individually wrapped
- ☐ spring-type clothespins
- ☐ craft sticks
- ☐ thin wooden dowel rods
- ☐ fabric ribbon, ½-inch wide
- ☐ dry florist moss
- ☐ cheerful greeting cards
- ☐ ice cream cones, flat-bottomed
- ☐ unshelled nuts or popcorn kernels
- ☐ 2 or 3-inch wide foam Christmas ball ornaments
- ☐ paper cups, plates, napkins
- ☐ lunch-size paper sacks
- ☐ plastic drinking straws
- ☐ plastic silverware
- ☐ pillow cases, solid light colors
- ☐ plastic milk jug or juice bottle caps
- ☐ red or green ½-inch pompons
- ☐ sandpaper sheets
- ☐ plastic lids from gallon-size detergent bottles or furniture polish cans
- ☐ plastic sandwich bags with zipper tops
- ☐ stickers, stars & religious themes
- ☐ 2 x 2-inch wood or foam blocks or empty spools
- ☐ yarn, thin & thick (red, blue, yellow, brown, black)
- ☐ 32-ounce yogurt or sour cream containers

Please bring the items on ______________________. *Thank you for your help!*

To Families of Four- and Five-Year-Olds

We have some exciting activities planned for use in teaching Bible lessons this year. Some of these crafts and projects utilize household items. We'd like to ask your help in saving these items for our activities. Here is a list of some of the items that we are collecting:

- ☐ adhesive-backed magnetic strips
- ☐ small adhesive bandages
- ☐ aluminum foil
- ☐ blue tissue paper
- ☐ 12 x 17-inch boxes or larger
- ☐ burger boxes from fast-food restaurants
- ☐ flat buttons
- ☐ taper candles
- ☐ large candy canes, individually wrapped
- ☐ spring-type clothespins
- ☐ craft sticks
- ☐ thin wooden dowel rods
- ☐ fabric ribbon, ½-inch wide
- ☐ dry florist moss
- ☐ cheerful greeting cards
- ☐ ice cream cones, flat-bottomed
- ☐ unshelled nuts or popcorn kernels
- ☐ 2 or 3-inch wide foam Christmas ball ornaments
- ☐ paper cups, plates, napkins
- ☐ lunch-size paper sacks
- ☐ plastic drinking straws
- ☐ plastic silverware
- ☐ pillow cases, solid light colors
- ☐ plastic milk jug or juice bottle caps
- ☐ red or green ½-inch pompons
- ☐ sandpaper sheets
- ☐ plastic lids from gallon-size detergent bottles or furniture polish cans
- ☐ plastic sandwich bags with zipper tops
- ☐ stickers, stars & religious themes
- ☐ 2 x 2-inch wood or foam blocks or empty spools
- ☐ yarn, thin & thick (red, blue, yellow, brown, black)
- ☐ 32-ounce yogurt or sour cream containers

Please bring the items on ______________________. *Thank you for your help!*

Abraham

Traveling Far from Home

Genesis 12:1-4; 13:14-18

Memory Verse

The Lord...blessed Abraham in all things.
Genesis 24:1

For the Teacher

Prior to class, sew the middle of a ½ x 36-inch piece of ribbon to the outside of the pillowcase seam, ten inches down from the open end. Write each child's name in permanent marker near the opening. Provide wide paintbrushes and toy buckets holding fabric paint (two parts water to one part paint) for the children to paint the pillowcases. When dry, pajamas may be stuffed inside and the bags may be tied with the ribbon. This may be an excellent time to give each child a small picture Bible as a gift.

Introduction

God told Abraham to leave his home and travel far away. God directed him where to go. Abraham obeyed God and God blessed him in many ways. At one point, God told Abraham to walk throughout the land of Canaan. God said all the land would one day belong to Abraham's family. Abraham moved his tents and followed God's direction. Perhaps he felt lonely at times, being away from his childhood home, but he always knew that God was with him.

Pillow Case Pajama Bag

Make a pajama bag to carry with you when you go somewhere overnight to visit. Paint a pillowcase with fabric paint and water using a wide brush. When it dries, pack your pajamas inside. Be sure to pack your Bible along with your pajamas! Before you go to sleep, you can look at the pictures in your Bible. This will help you remember that even though your bedroom or family might be far away, God is always with you.

HINT: When a project involves messy hands, provide ample clean-up supplies. Have a bucket of water, towels, and a trash container within several steps of the work area. Wear paint smocks and cover work surfaces with disposable paper or plastic shower curtains.

Finished Pajama Bag

Abraham

Father of Many Nations

Genesis 17:1-10

Memory Verse

You will be the father of many nations.
Genesis 17:4 (NIV)

For the Teacher

Duplicate a pattern page for each child. Cut two slits in each paper. Help the children slide a large candy cane or bent chenille wire through the slits for a staff. Tape the back to hold the staff in place. Discuss positive attributes of parents as the children work.

Introduction

Abraham's name used to be Abram. One day God changed it! God told Abram that his new name would be Abraham because he would become the father of many nations. This was a very special honor God gave to Abraham. It was through this one man and his family that the Israelite nation was formed.

Father Abraham

Color the picture of Abraham. Give him a shepherd's staff to hold. You can give this picture as a present to your father or mother. Remember that God is your heavenly Father. He watches you grow, helps protect you, and helps you have the things you need.

Abraham, the father of many nations

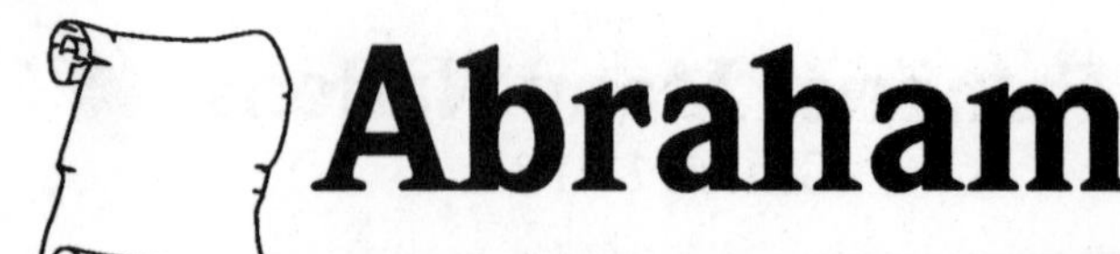

Abraham

Promised Many Descendants

Genesis 15:2-6

Memory Verse

He Who promised is faithful.
Hebrews 10:23 (NIV)

For the Teacher

Duplicate a picture for each child. Provide yellow tempera paints in shallow dishes. Demonstrate how to dip one finger into the paint and make yellow dots in the sky. Explain that God gave Abraham a promise that seemed impossible. Nevertheless, God always keeps His promises.

Introduction

Abraham felt sad. He did not have any children. One day God took Abraham outside his tent and told him to look up into the night sky. Abraham looked up and saw millions of twinkling stars. Next, God promised that Abraham would have as many children and grandchildren and great-grandchildren as there were stars. Even though it seemed impossible, Abraham believed in God's promise.

Fingerprint Stars

Dip your pointer finger into yellow paint. Carefully paint yellow dots to fill up the sky with stars. When you're finished try to count how many stars you made. Are there too many to count? Now you know how Abraham felt when God told him how many relatives he would have.

He Who promised is faithful. —Hebrews 10:23 (NIV)

Abraham

A True Test of Love

Genesis 22:1-19

Memory Verse

We ought to obey God.
Acts 5:29

For the Teacher

Duplicate a picture for each child. Tell the story and help the children find the sheep. Provide tiny bits of cotton and glue sticks. Help the children spread the glue and then add the cotton. Let them color the other hidden animals green to match the bushes. Talk about the animals as the children find them.

Introduction

God decided to test Abraham to see if Abraham loved his son Isaac more than God. God told Abraham to bring Isaac to a mountain and sacrifice (or kill) the boy. Abraham obeyed God by bringing Isaac to the mountain. Just when he was ready to sacrifice his son, an angel told Abraham, "Stop." Abraham sacrificed a sheep instead. This story shows us that Abraham loved God most of all.

Find the Sheep

Help Abraham find the sheep in the bushes. Glue a piece of cotton on the sheep when you find it. Then, color the picture green. As you color, think of ways you can show God you love Him. Say, "Thank You, God, for giving me the Bible so that I can learn how to love You more."

Joseph

Part of God's Special Plan

Genesis 45:1-8

Memory Verse

God works for the good of those who love Him.
Romans 8:28 (NIV)

For the Teacher

Before class, duplicate and cut out a memory verse for each child. Cut paper plates in half, one half per child. Draw eyes on the plates, using the bottom of the plate as the front of the face. Help each child add a craft stick handle. Reinforce with clear tape, if necessary. After the children decorate their masks, play a game. Have one child stand beside you with her mask. Ask the remaining children, **Is this Patsy?** Suggest the wrong name. Repeat several times. Then say the right name. Say, **Thank You God for Kendra. Help her trust that You will work out a wonderful plan for her life.**

Introduction

Joseph loved God. When his father gave him a beautiful coat, it made his brothers mad. Joseph's brothers sold him into slavery. Later, Joseph went to prison because someone told a lie about him. When Joseph finally saw his brothers again, they did not even recognize him. Yet, Joseph knew that God cared for him. Joseph believed that God was able to use the things that happened to him in His wonderful plan. Because of Joseph and his relationship with God, many people were saved from starvation, including his very own family.

Guess Who?

You can make a mask to play a guessing game with your friends. Keep the straight edge of the paper plate towards the bottom. Glue a craft stick down from the center to form a handle. Decorate your mask with feathers, crepe paper, yarn, sequins, and other scraps. Cut out the memory verse and glue it on the back. When dry, grasp the craft stick and hold the mask in front of your face.

HINT: Four- and five-year-olds are learning how to take turns. When an activity involves this skill, speak patiently with the children. Reassure them by saying, **Each of you will get a turn. Please wait quietly so that I may call on you.**

God works for the good of those who love Him.
— Romans 8:28 (NIV)

Finished Mask

Joseph

An Amazing Life Story

Genesis 42:1-46:3

Memory Verse

The Lord was with Joseph and gave him success.
Genesis 39:23 (NIV)

For the Teacher

Duplicate one set of cards from pages 13 and 14 and cut them apart. Glue the small cards on the back of the appropriate picture cards. Cover the cards with clear adhesive-backed plastic. Provide at least ten plastic milk or juice bottle caps for each child. Work slowly with the group, allowing ample time to collect the lids.

Introduction

Bring the story of Joseph to life with this counting game. Review the major events of Joseph's life and practice counting at the same time! To play, place plastic milk or juice bottle caps in the center of the table. The teacher will show one card and read the description on the back. Collect the matching number of bottle caps as the teacher reads. After each card, the teacher will choose one child and will count his lids slowly out loud.

Can You Count for Joseph?

As your teacher shows you a card, pick out the matching number of lids to place in a pile in front of your seat. Your teacher will help you count them to see if you are correct. Then, push these lids back into the center and wait for your teacher to show you another card.

1 Coat: Joseph's father gave him a colorful coat.	**6 Prisoners:** In jail, Joseph was put in charge of all the other prisoners.
2 Stars: Joseph dreamed that the stars bowed down to him.	**7 Cows:** Pharaoh got Joseph out of prison to explain his dream about seven cows.
3 Sheep: Joseph's father sent him to find his brothers, who were tending sheep.	**8 Gifts:** Joseph explained the dream, so Pharaoh put him in charge of the land and gave him gifts.
4 Camels: Joseph's brothers sold him to slave traders passing by on camels.	**9 Barns:** Joseph stored food in many barns to survive during the famine.
5 Coins: As a slave, Joseph was put in charge of all his master's money.	**10 Brothers:** Ten of Joseph's brothers came to Joseph asking for food. God brought the family back together.

3
4
5
6
7
8
9
10

Joseph

Doing His Best All the Time

Genesis 39:1-5, 20-23

Memory Verse

Let us do good unto all.
Galatians 6:10

For the Teacher

Duplicate the poem pattern for each child and cut it out. Spray paint the ice-cream cones with clear acrylic paint before class, one cone per child. Emphasize that these craft cones are not safe to eat. Provide one decorated 2- or 3-inch foam Christmas ball, one ½-inch red or green pompon, and a 12-inch length of ribbon for each cone. After the craft, it might be fun to have an ice-cream cone party as a tasty treat. Explain the concept of the craft to the parents or send home a short note.

Introduction

Even when Joseph was a slave and in prison, he did his very best. His warden saw that Joseph always did his best and put him in charge of the other prisoners. This ice-cream cone craft can be kept in the kitchen cupboard for special occasions. When the family wants to honor a member's accomplishments, the cone can sit by that person's plate during a meal as a special treat.

A Special Treat

Glue a decorated foam ball on the top of the ice-cream cone. Glue a pompon on the top of the ball to look like a cherry. Color the border around the poem. Your teacher will help you tie a ribbon around the cone to attach the poem. Take this treat home and show it to your family. When someone has a special day, you can place the cone next to his plate during dinner to show that you share in his happiness.

HINT: Keep in mind that a craft for a four- or five-year-old is an important learning experience. It is best to encourage the children to complete the project themselves. Allow for expressions of creativity and individuality as the activity is accomplished.

Finished Treat

Moses

Hidden in the Reeds

Exodus 2:1-10

Memory Verse

Trust in the Lord.
Proverbs 3:5

For the Teacher

Duplicate a Moses picture for each child and cut it out. Demonstrate how to place 1-inch pieces of blue tissue paper on construction paper and brush starch over each piece until the construction paper is covered. As it dries, let the children color the Moses picture and glue it on top of the tissue paper. Say, **Think about how Moses' mother trusted God. When everything seemed hopeless, she knew that God would work out the best situation for her baby boy.** Let the children talk about times they have trusted an adult. Explain that God wants our trust, also.

Introduction

Pharaoh decided to kill the Israelite baby boys. One mother hid her son from Pharaoh's evil plan. When her son grew too big to hide, she put him in a special basket and floated him on the Nile river, hidden in the reeds and grasses. The mother trusted that God would take care of her baby. Pharaoh's daughter found the floating baby and adopted him as her son. She named him Moses.

The Floating Basket

Help baby Moses float on the water. Use a paint brush to brush starch over each piece of tissue paper until a construction paper sheet is covered, resembling the river. Color the picture of Moses and glue him on the river. As you work, think of how Moses' mother trusted God.

Finished Picture

Moses

Following God's Plan

Exodus 12-40; Deuteronomy 1-30

Memory Verse

"I know the plans I have for you," declares the Lord.
Jeremiah 29:11 (NIV)

For the Teacher

Duplicate a picture of one Israelite for each child to color and eventually hang at random on the map mural. On the floor, spread a piece of poster paper large enough to cover a bulletin board. Supply toy cars and tempera paints in shallow containers. Let the children paint tracks on the paper. When dry, draw Moses, Mount Sinai, the burning bush, the Jordan River, the Promised Land, and the Red Sea.

Introduction

When Moses led the Israelites out from Egypt, God had a plan for their lives. Even though they wandered in the desert for forty years, as if for no reason, God's plan was being accomplished. God has an important plan for each of our lives, just as He had a plan for the Israelites.

A Map of God's Plan

Dip toy cars in paint and take turns driving them around on the paper to make painted pathways. This is a reminder of how the Israelites wandered in the wilderness. Your teacher will make this painting into a map mural and hang it on the wall for you to look at as you learn about Moses. Color and cut out an Israelite to add to the map when it dries.

Finished Mural

Moses

Heading Toward the Promised Land

Exodus 12:31- 20

Memory Verse

Fear not: for I am with thee.
Isaiah 43:5

For the Teacher

Duplicate pattern pages 18 and 19 for each child. Glue the pages to poster board. Cut the pieces apart and store each set in a zipper plastic sandwich bag. Cut red yarn into 2-inch lengths and blue yarn into 3-inch lengths, several for each child. Cut two foil tablets for each child using the Ten Commandments outline as a guide.

Introduction

Through Moses, God led the Israelites away from Egypt and slavery. Pharaoh chased them, but they crossed the Red Sea safely. God gave Moses the Ten Commandments on the top of Mount Sinai while the Israelites camped at the bottom. On their journey to the Promised Land, God led them with a cloud by day and a pillar of fire by night. God was with Moses, and God is with us, too.

A Magnetic Story

Make magnets to tell this story of the Israelites. Color the pictures of the people. Glue red yarn on the fire, blue yarn on the sea, cotton on the cloud, a button on the chariot wheel, florist moss on the mountain, fabric scraps on the people, and foil on the tablets. Attach a ½-inch magnetic strip behind each picture.

Mount Sinai
Ten Commandments
Cloud by Day
Fire by Night
Pharaoh
Red Sea

Joshua

The Fall of Jericho

Joshua 6

Memory Verse

The Lord strong and mighty.
Psalm 24:8

For the Teacher

Duplicate one memory verse box for each child. Prior to class, make six wooden or foam blocks per child. Each block should be a 2 x 2-inch square. Sand rough corners to prevent splinters. Provide tempera paint and brushes for the children to use. Allow the blocks to dry on waxed paper. While making the craft help the children understand that God Himself made the wall of Jericho tumble down.

Introduction

When Joshua led his army against the walled city of Jericho, how did the wall fall down? Did the soldiers knock it over? No. The Israelites simply followed God's direction to march, play the trumpets, and shout. God, Himself, used His mighty strength to make Jericho's walls crumble to the ground. God is the most powerful force in the world!

The Wall of Jericho

Paint several blocks and glue the memory verse on one of them. When dry, you can play a stacking game with a friend. Take turns trying to stack all the blocks. For extra fun, save the block with the memory verse for the very top. If you can do this without letting them fall over, you win the game! Then, say the memory verse, push the blocks down, and start the game over again.

HINT: If wood or foam are not available, use empty spools of thread. Instead of painting, the children may decorate them with stickers.

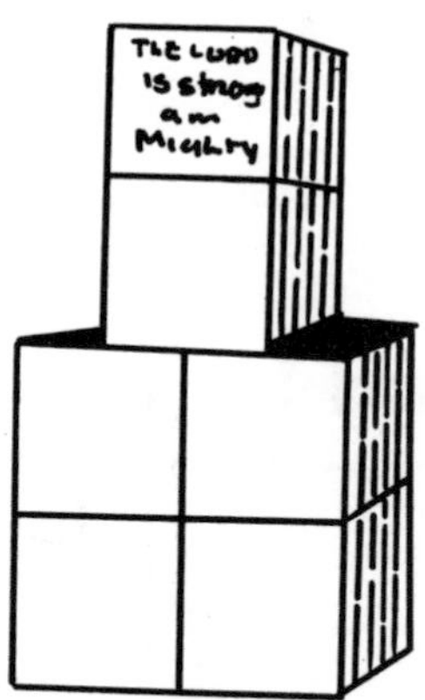

Six Completed Blocks

The Lord is strong and mighty.	**The Lord is strong and mighty.**	**The Lord is strong and mighty.**	**The Lord is strong and mighty.**

Joshua

Spies Go into the Promised Land

Joshua 2:1-21

Memory Verse

The Lord will protect him.
Psalm 41:2 (NIV)

For the Teacher

Duplicate the patterns for each child and cut them out. Thread a 12-inch length of yarn through a paper clip. After each child glues a building onto paper, place the yarn so it extends from one dot to the other. Tape the top and bottom of the yarn about one inch above and below the dots. Place glue on the broken lines and let the children glue the flax to the top of the roof.

Introduction

Joshua sent two spies into the Promised Land. The spies' lives were in danger after the king discovered their plot. Rahab hid the two men under bundles of flax on her rooftop until it was safe. She then helped them escape down a rope. For this bravery her family was saved when Jericho was destroyed.

Hidden Spies

Color the pictures. Glue the building to a piece of construction paper. Tape a paper clip to the back of the spies. Your teacher will help you tape and glue the picture together. When finished, hide the spies under the flax, then lower them to safety. Read the memory verse on the picture. We can trust God to protect us just as He used Rahab to protect the spies.

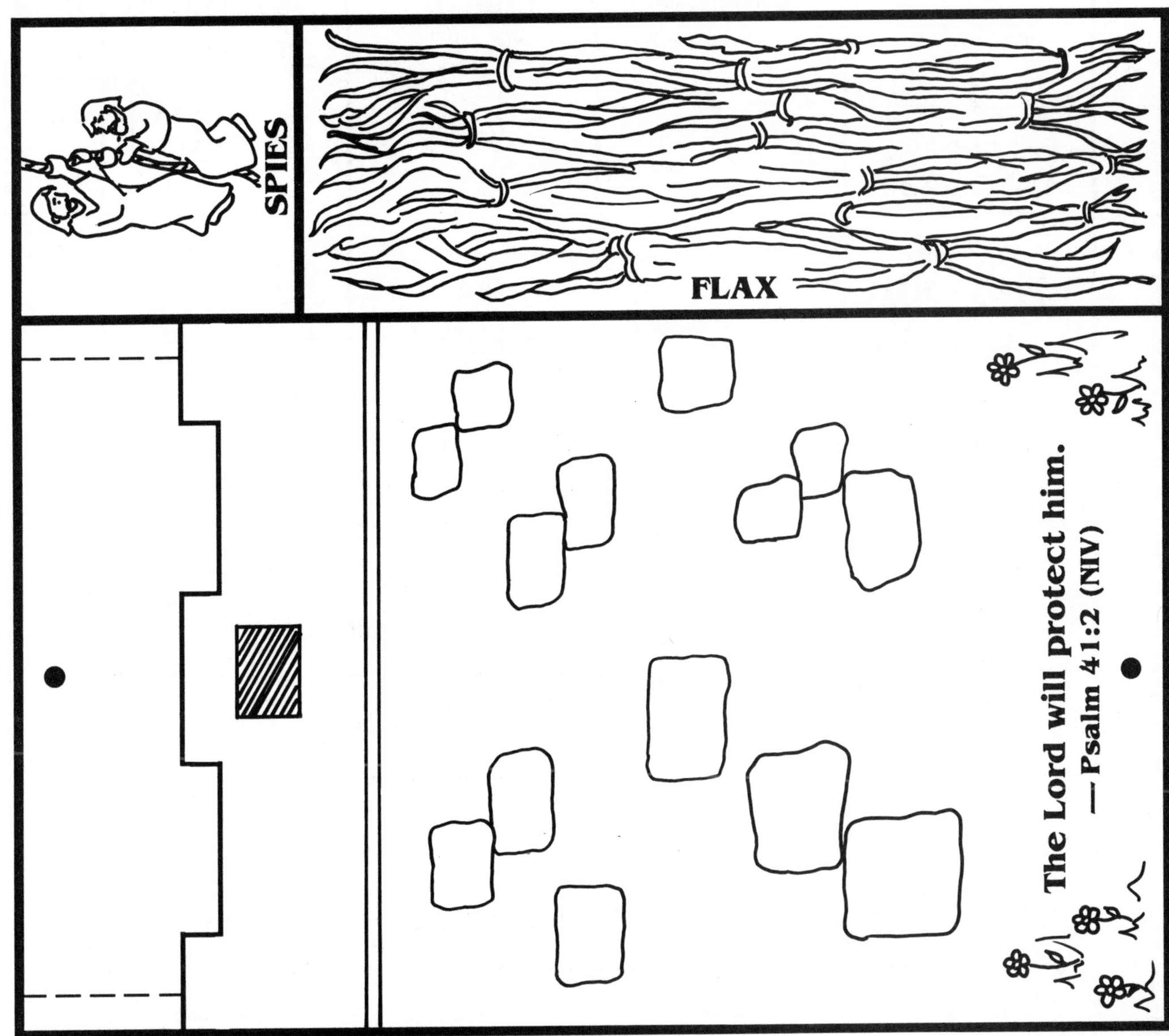

Joshua

Following God's Directions

Joshua 6

Memory Verse

Do what the Lord has commanded.
Joshua 8:8 (NIV)

For the Teacher

Before class, duplicate a copy of pages 22 and 23 for each child. Glue the patterns to poster board. Spread the glue with a paint brush to cover the edges completely. Cut out the dominoes when dry. Store each set in a self-closing plastic sandwich bag. Let each child color a set. Explain how to play the game.

Introduction

The Lord told Joshua that He would deliver Jericho into Joshua's hands. He gave specific directions for Joshua and the Israelites to follow. He told them to march around the city with all the guards, carrying the ark and blowing trumpets. Afterwards, the walls of Jericho fell completely down.

Dominoes

Make a domino game. Color each picture. Divide the dominoes among the players. Lay the picture of Joshua in the center. Moving from left to right, let each player add dominoes, carefully matching the pictures, until he has no more matches. Tell the story of Joshua as you play. The first person to use all his dominoes wins the game.

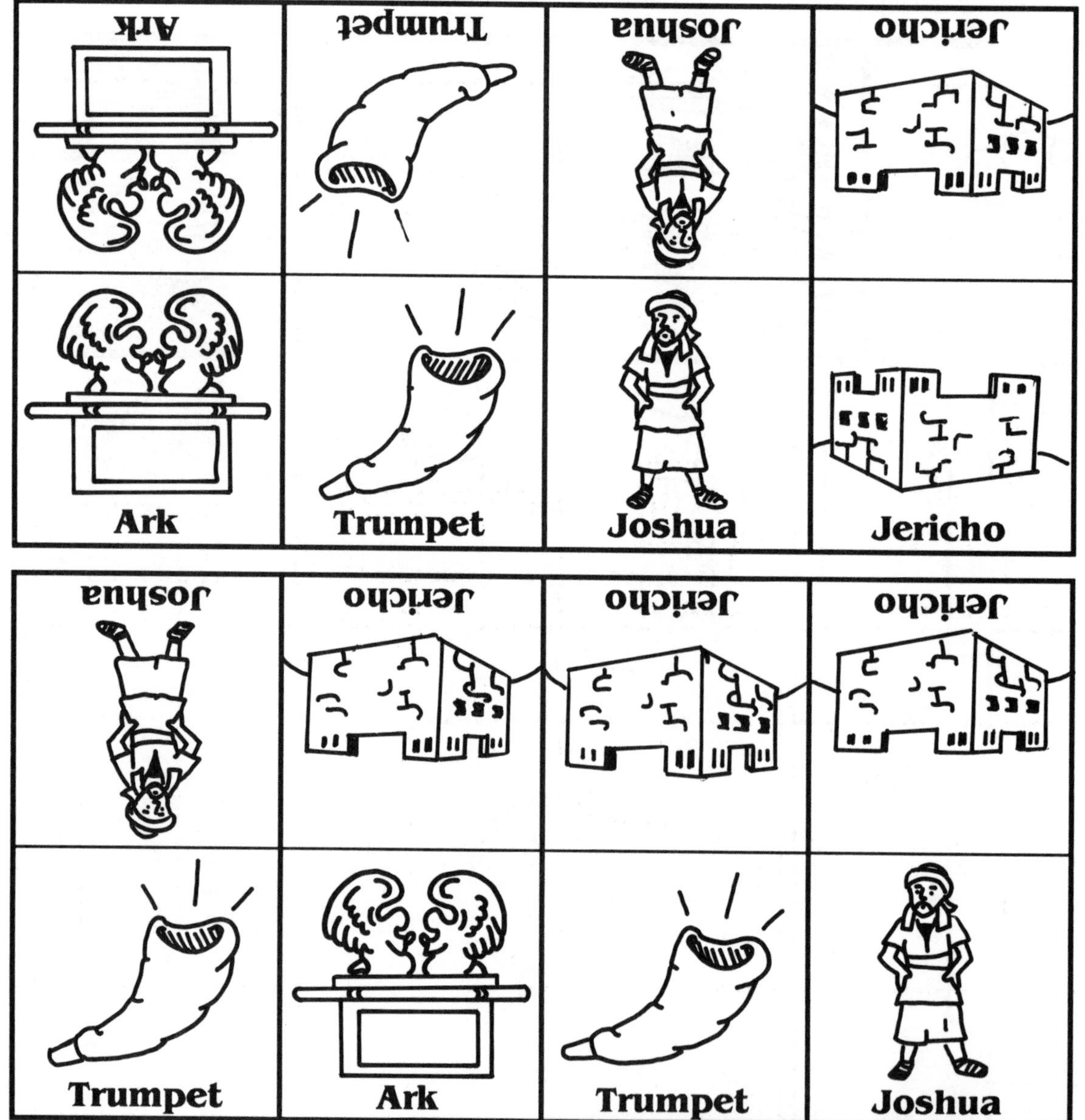

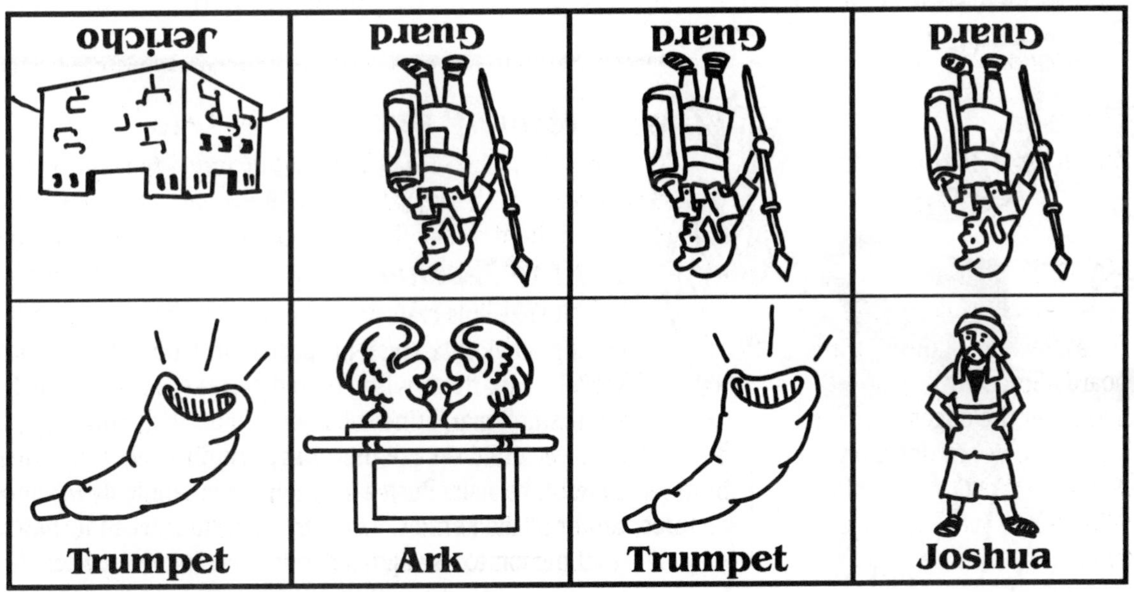
Jericho
Guard
Guard
Guard
Trumpet
Ark
Trumpet
Joshua

Jericho
Guard
Trumpet
Joshua
Guard
Guard
Ark
Ark

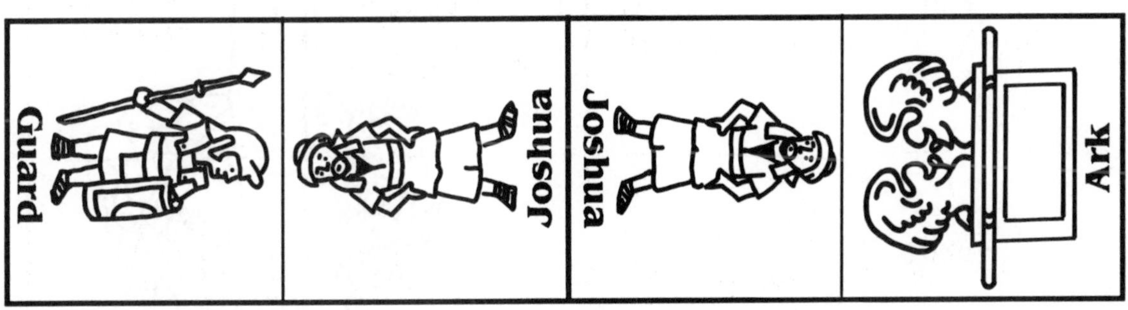
Guard
Joshua
Joshua
Ark

Ruth

Helping Her Mother-in-Law

Ruth 1:14-18

Memory Verse

Let us love one another.
I John 4:7

For the Teacher

NOTE: This craft will take three days to dry. In a large mixing bowl, mix an all-purpose craft glue with popcorn kernels. Mix them with colored corn kernels for added color. Spray small margarine tubs with a non-stick vegetable coating. Help the children use their hands to fill a tub with glue-covered kernels. Push a 10-inch taper candle down into the center of the kernels. The kernels form the candle base and hold the candle straight. Remove the Harvest Candle from the tub when dry, in about three days.

Introduction

Naomi, her husband, and two sons moved from Bethlehem to Moab during a famine. Both sons married. One son married Ruth. Eventually, Naomi's husband and two sons died. Naomi decided to return to Bethlehem. She encouraged Ruth to go back to her own home. Ruth loved Naomi and didn't want to leave her. In a beautiful speech, Ruth explained her love for Naomi and God.

Harvest Candle

Ruth told her mother-in-law of her love for her. You can tell someone of your love for them, too! While you make this pretty candle, think of the person you would like to give it to as a gift. Think of the words you will say when you present it. Take time to thank God for this person. Pray, "Thank You, God, for the love I have for her."

HINT: White glue may be used instead of all-purpose craft glue. However, the candle holder will take longer to dry and will be less shiny. Small buttons, seashells, or unshelled nuts make a unique alternative to popcorn kernels.

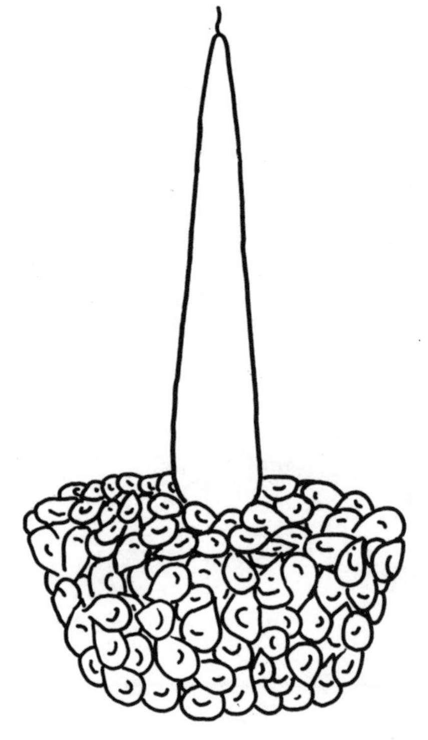

Completed Candle

Ruth

Being Kind to Naomi & Boaz

Ruth 1-4

Memory Verse

Thou hast shown...kindness.
Ruth 3:10

For the Teacher

Duplicate a picture of Ruth for each child. Duplicate the puppet pattern onto poster board, two per child. Punch holes around the curved edges, one inch apart. Cut yarn into 3-foot lengths. Wrap tape around one end of each yarn piece. Help each child tape the yarn at the flat end of the puppet. Show her how to sew the poster board together. Help her knot the other end when completed.

Introduction

Ruth lived in the country of Moab with Naomi, her mother-in-law. When Naomi decided to return to her home town of Bethlehem, Ruth begged to accompany her. Together they traveled to Bethlehem where Ruth harvested barley for food. Ruth eventually married Boaz and became the great-grandmother of King David.

Ruth Hand Puppet

Your teacher will show you how to sew this puppet of Ruth. Color the picture of Ruth and glue it on the poster board. Put it on your hand to tell a story about Ruth. Move your hand forward to show Ruth following Naomi to Bethlehem. Bend your hand down to show Ruth harvesting grain from the barley field. Pretend that Ruth marries Boaz.

HINT: Chenille wire is often easier for young children to thread through holes. Use several wires for each puppet. Tape the wire ends when finished.

Completed Puppet

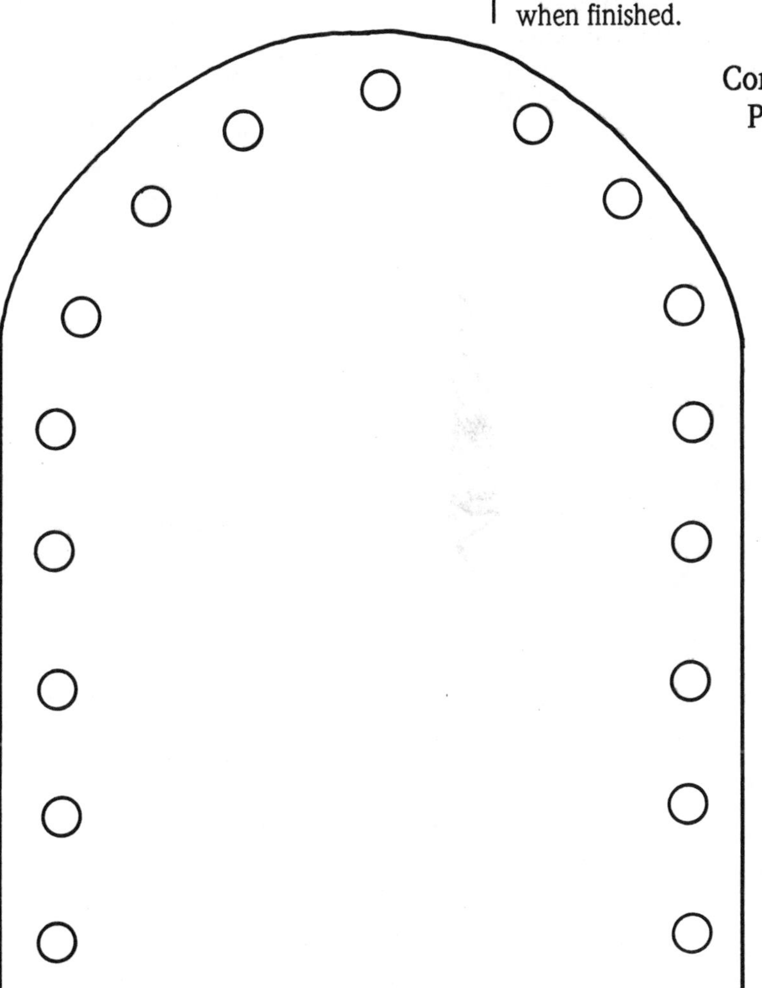

Ruth

God Took Care of Her

Ruth 1-4

Memory Verse

God will meet all your needs.
Philippians 4:19 (NIV)

For the Teacher

Duplicate the pattern page for each child. Discuss the different types of foods, explaining which ones are made from grains. Provide a sample of the various foods to taste. Help the children draw lines with the glue from the grain to the foods. Let them place an uncooked spaghetti noodle on each line of glue. Say the memory verse together as they work.

Introduction

This story of Ruth demonstrates how God took care of her. He protected her by leading her to the safety of Boaz' fields. He provided food for her when Boaz generously allowed her to harvest the barley and wheat. He established a wonderful future for Ruth through her marriage with Boaz and the birth of her son. This story gives us encouragement that God will also meet our own needs.

The Guessing Game

God provided Ruth with food by giving her an opportunity to work in the barley and wheat fields. Look at this picture and try to guess what kind of food can be made from barley and wheat. Glue spaghetti noodles to make connecting lines from the center picture of barley and wheat to the pictures of the foods made of barley and wheat.

God will meet all your needs. — Philippians 4:19 (NIV)

Ruth

Setting a Good Example

Ruth 1-4

Memory Verse

Set...an example by doing what is good.
Titus 2:7 (NIV)

For the Teacher

Duplicate and cut out a memory verse for each child. Also provide the following for each child: an 11 x 17-inch construction paper sheet, a paper plate, a paper cup, a paper napkin, a plastic fork, a plastic spoon, and a plastic knife. Help the children glue the place setting onto the piece of paper. Provide dry macaroni noodles and dry beans or rice for the children to glue on the plate. A box of raisins may be added as a treat. The children can eat the raisins and glue on the empty box.

Introduction

Ruth sets a wonderful example for us today. She worked hard in the harvest fields. She was polite and kind. She took on the responsibility of caring for the members of her family. She provided food for Naomi. She followed Naomi's advice to marry Boaz according to the custom of the law.

The Harvest Meal

Ruth worked hard to provide food for her family. You can share in the mealtime work at your house, too. Your teacher will show you how to glue the place setting in its proper order. Just for fun, you can also glue some food on the plate. When you return home, you can help set the table for your family by following your craft as a guide.

Completed Meal

Set . . . an example by doing what is good.

— Titus 2:7 (NIV)

Elijah

A Prophet of God

I Kings 17-19; II Kings 2

Memory Verse

He did what the Lord had told him.
I Kings 17:5 (NIV)

For the Teacher

Duplicate pattern pages 28 and 29 and cut apart the strips so that each child has one strip. Write each of the following sets of words on separate index cards, one phrase per card: Elijah: a prophet of God; Rain: God told Elijah it wouldn't rain for several years; Raven: The ravens brought food to Elijah during the drought; Oil: God filled a widow's jars with oil; Fire: Fire fell from heaven to prove that the Lord is God; Cloak: Elijah gave his cloak to the next prophet, Elisha; Chariot: God sent a chariot of fire and carried Elijah to heaven in a whirlwind. Provide four plastic lids from milk jugs or juice bottles for each child. Shuffle the index cards and randomly read each picture's description.

Introduction

Elijah was a prophet of God. During his lifetime, God performed many miracles. These miracles helped the Israelites believe in the holy power of God.

Miracle Bingo

As your teacher calls out the description of different pictures, check your bingo sheet carefully. If you find the picture on your sheet, cover it with a plastic lid. If your sheet does not have that picture, wait until your teacher calls out the next one. The first person to cover all four pictures on the bingo sheet wins the game.

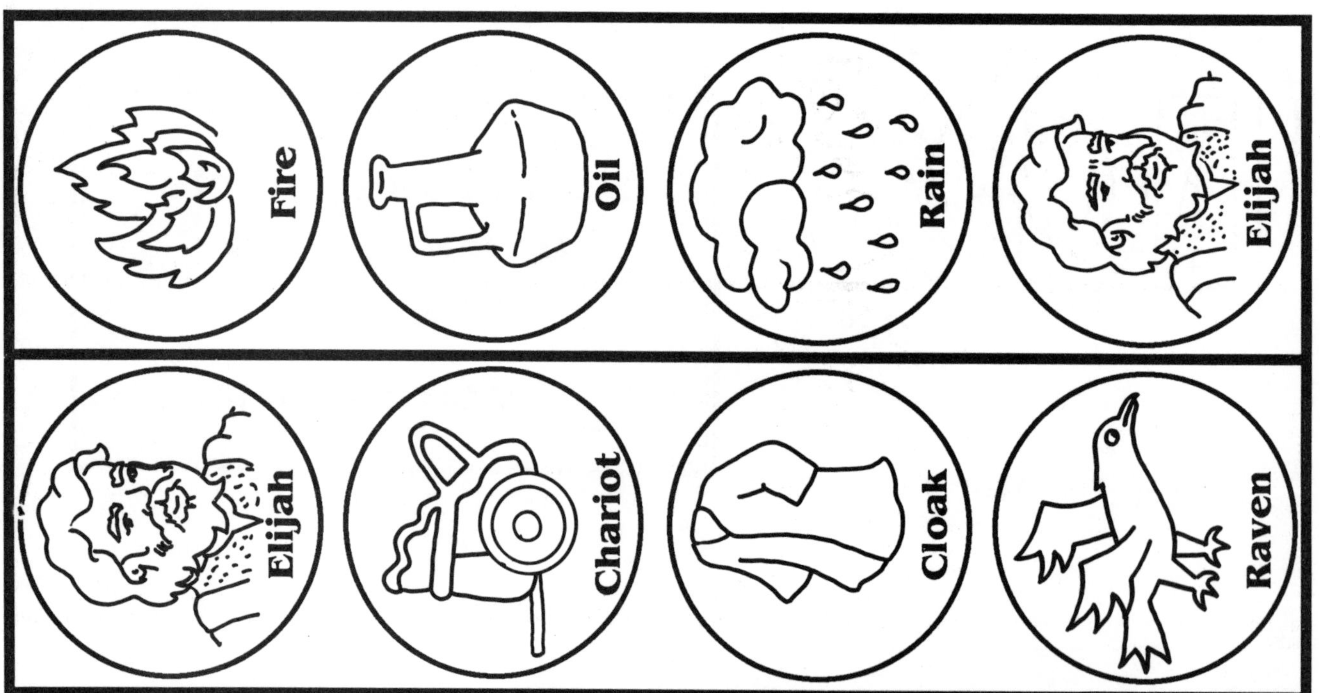

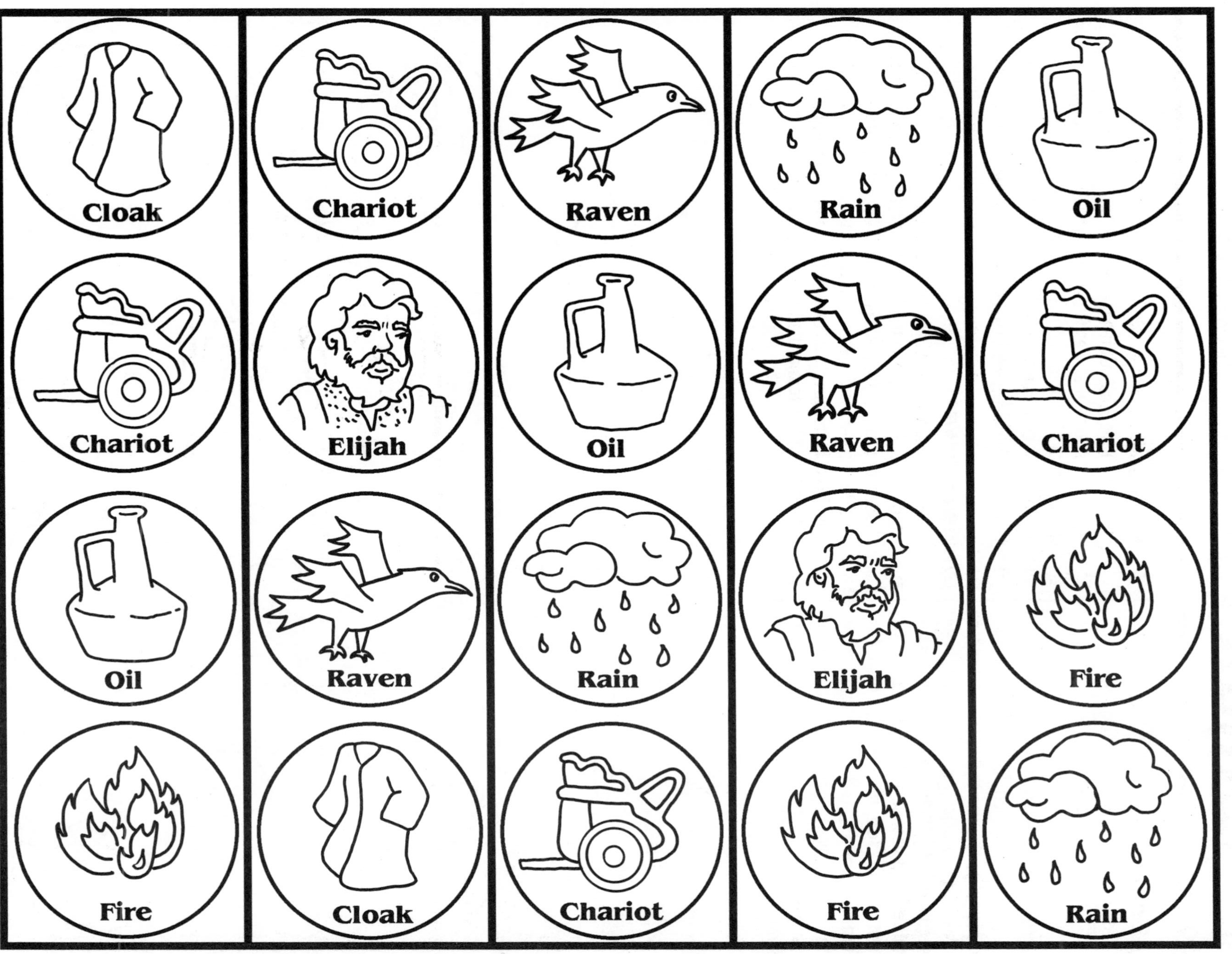
Cloak
Chariot
Raven
Rain
Oil
Chariot
Elijah
Oil
Raven
Chariot
Oil
Raven
Rain
Elijah
Fire
Fire
Cloak
Chariot
Fire
Rain

Elijah

Talking to God

I Kings 17:1-4

Memory Verse

The Lord will hear when I call unto Him.
Psalm 4:3

For the Teacher

Duplicate a picture for each child. Encourage the children to find the five hidden crowns by themselves and glue a large sequin or piece of foil on each. Say, **Elijah talked and listened to God. Each of us can talk to God, too. We can hear His Words to us as we listen to them from the Bible.** Say a prayer asking God to help us take time to pray and listen to Bible stories.

Introduction

Elijah gave King Ahab God's message. Elijah warned the king of the terrible dry season that was to come. Then God told Elijah to hide by a special brook. Elijah did what God told him to do. This story shows that Elijah could talk freely with God. It reminds us that we should spending time talking to God in prayer, too.

Hidden Crowns

Color the picture of Elijah praying beside the brook. God had instructed him to hide here so that the king and queen would not kill him. Hidden in this picture are five crowns. Try to find them while you color. When you find the crowns, glue a gold or silver piece on each one. You can hang this picture in your room to remind you to pray to God about the things that happen in your life.

Elijah

An Important Message from God

1 Kings 18:1-2

Memory Verse

The Lord is King for ever.
Psalm 10:16

For the Teacher

Duplicate a scepter pattern and a construction paper circle this same size for each scepter. For each crown, cut a piece of 11 x 17-inch paper in half lengthwise to form points. Tape the two halves together in the center. Size a crown on each student's head. Cut off the excess paper. Lay the crown flat to decorate. When finished, tape the ends together to fit each child's head.

Introduction

The Israelite people were not following God. They were worshipping idols instead. God sent Elijah to tell King Ahab of the terrible mistake everyone was making. Unfortunately, King Ahab and his wicked wife Queen Jezebel, did not listen to Elijah. They chose to ignore his words. They continued doing evil in the sight of the Lord.

The Ruling Scepter

Decorate your scepter and crown to make them fancy. Use glue to add sequins, wrapping paper pieces, and foil to the crown. For the scepter, glue a straw and several streamers between the paper circles. Decorate the scepter to match your crown. Think about the things you would do if you were king or queen. How could your laws help the people obey God instead of following the crowd?

The Lord is King for ever. — Psalm 10:16

Scepter Pattern

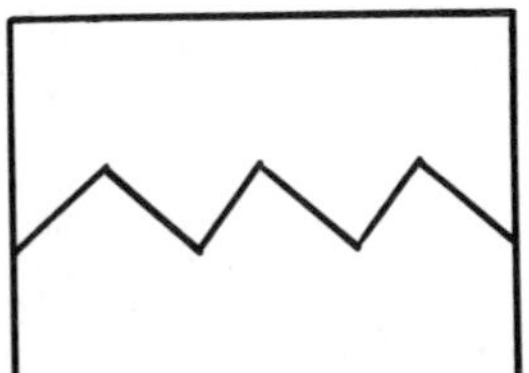

Completed Scepter and Crown

Cut crown

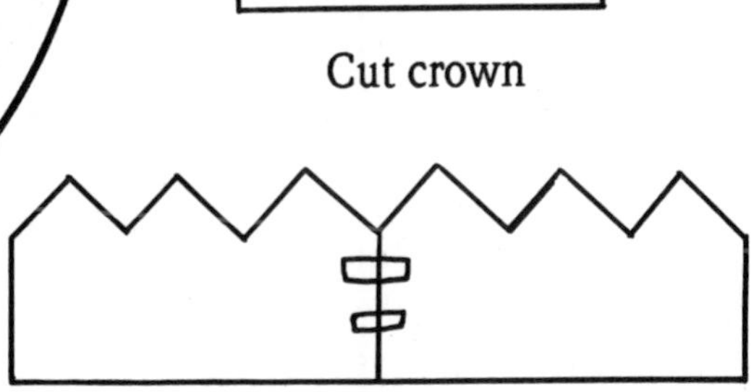

Tape

Shadrach

Three Men Worship God

Daniel 3

Memory Verse

The Lord is...the great King above all gods.
Psalm 95:3 (NIV)

For the Teacher

You will need pattern pages 32, 33, and 34. Duplicate the memory verse, poem, and puppet people on regular weight typing paper. Duplicate the flames on red, orange, and yellow construction paper, six flames per child. Duplicate two crowns for each child using yellow construction paper. Cut the following from poster board for each child: one hand, one strap, and one theater. Staple the strap to the back of the hand, covering the staples with clear tape for safety.

Introduction

Shadrach, Meshach, and Abednego knew that God was king above all earthly kings. They chose to worship God instead of bowing down to King Nebuchadnezzar. As the children repeat this poem, they will be reminded that God is a wonderful King. They can share this message with their family and friends as they perform the play.

Fiery Furnace Theater

Color and glue the puppets on the end of the fingers (front side of the hand), being careful to put the king on the thumb and the angel on the pinkie. Glue six flames across the top of the theater. Glue two crowns on the front and decorate with sequins. Glue the memory verse on the front. Tape the poem on the back right side of the theater.

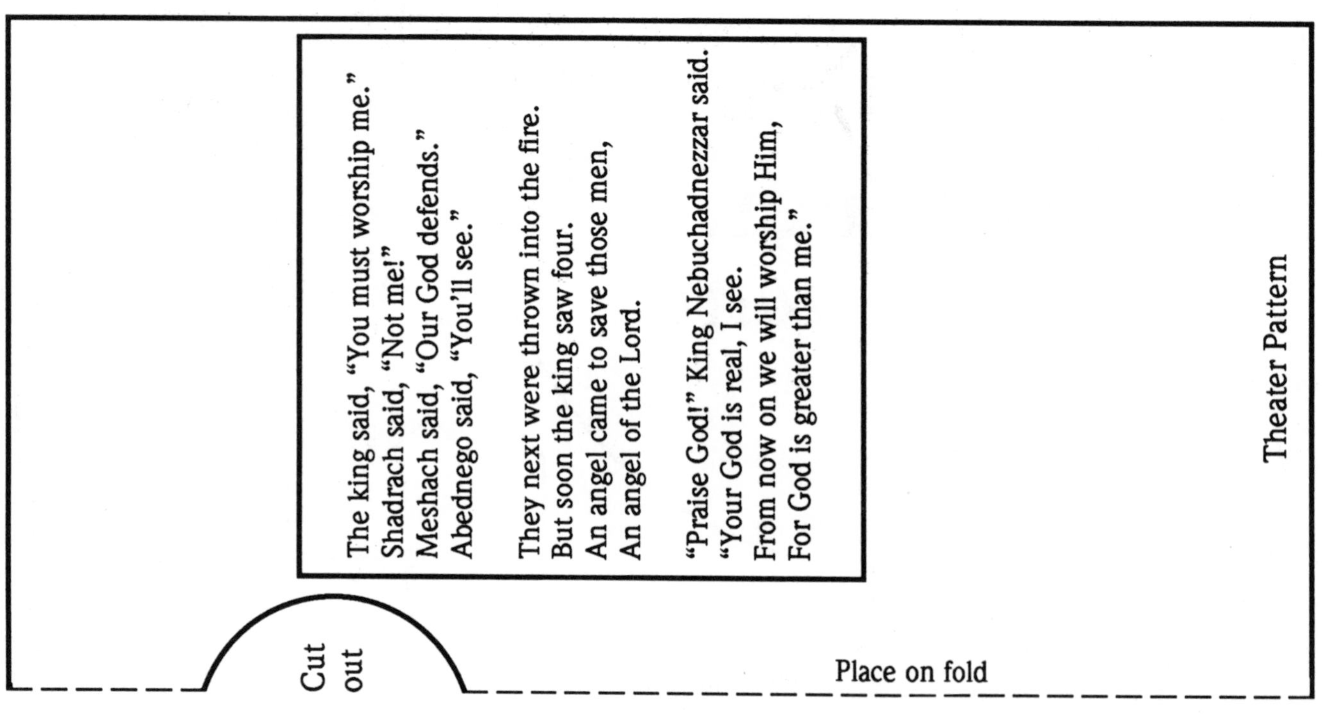

The Lord is . . .
the great King above
all gods.
— Psalm 95:3

Completed Theater

Strap Pattern

Shadrach

Eating Good Food
Daniel 1:11-16

Memory Verse
Eat what is good.
Isaiah 55:2 (NIV)

For the Teacher
Cut two 4 x 5-inch paper pockets. Draw a frowning face on one pocket and glue it to a large poster board sheet to hold the 2 ¼-inch cards. Draw a smiling face on the other pocket and glue it to hold the 2-inch cards so the larger cards do not fit. Duplicate, color, and cut a card for each child. Glue the cards onto poster board. Give each child a card and let him put it in the correct pocket.

Introduction
Shadrach, Meshach, and Abednego were taken to Babylon. In order to prepare to serve the king, they were offered rich food and wine. Instead, these men chose to eat vegetables and water. When they were later examined, they were healthier than the people who ate the king's food. This story demonstrates the importance of choosing healthy foods to eat.

Good Food Pocket Game
Think about the food you eat. Some food is good to eat and makes you healthy. Some food is called junk food. Your body does not really need this kind of food. You can be like Shadrach, Meshach, and Abednego. You can choose healthy food to eat. When you play the pocket game, place the healthy food in the smiling face pocket and the junk food in the frowning face pocket.

HINT: Pictures of various foods can be cut from magazines and newspapers, glued to construction paper, and covered with clear adhesive-backed plastic. Cut the healthy food into 2-inch squares and the unhealthy food into 2 ¼-inch squares.

Jonah

Praying for God's Forgiveness

Jonah 2:1-2

Memory Verse

From inside the fish Jonah prayed.
Jonah 2:1 (NIV)

For the Teacher

Duplicate the pattern page for each child. NOTE: The Jonah pattern is also used with the Road to Nineveh on page 38. Draw the outline of a fish on the side of a large box, one box per child. Provide tempera paint and brushes for the children to paint the fish. Help them cut out and glue the memory verse on the box and glue Jonah on the fish's tummy. Encourage the children to say a prayer and talk to God each time they play with the box.

Introduction

God told Jonah to go to the city of Nineveh. Jonah decided to ignore God and go traveling on a ship instead. While on the ship, a terrible storm blew all around. Jonah was tossed overboard and swallowed up by a huge fish. Stuck inside the fish for three days, Jonah prayed to God. God heard Jonah's prayer for forgiveness and answered it by making the fish spit Jonah up on the beach.

Prayer Box

Use a paintbrush to paint the fish picture on a large box. Glue Jonah inside the fish. Glue the memory verse on the box. Then, climb inside the box and pretend you are Jonah. Close your eyes and pray to God. Ask Him to forgive you for something you may have done that wasn't the best thing to do. Thank Him for His forgiveness. Open your eyes and pretend you are swimming around inside a great big fish!

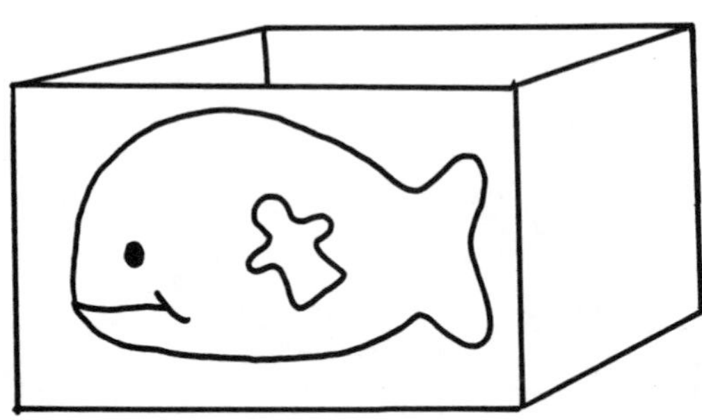

Completed Box

From inside the fish Jonah prayed.

— Jonah 2:1 (NIV)

Jonah

Obeying God's Words
Jonah 2-3

Memory Verse
Obey the Lord your God.
Deuteronomy 27:10 (NIV)

For the Teacher
Duplicate a pattern for each child. Provide crayons, glue sticks and poster board. After they color and glue the puzzle, help the children cut it. Point to the letters on the patterns and slowly say each word. Discuss the importance of obedience. Ask the children to describe times when they chose to obey their parents.

Introduction
Jonah disobeyed God when he decided not to visit Nineveh. After he was swallowed by the fish, Jonah realized that it was best to obey. He asked God to forgive his disobedience. Jonah then promised to obey God's words. It is important to obey God. It is also important to obey our parents and teachers.

Fish Fun Word Puzzle
Make a fun puzzle and learn how to spell! Color the picture of Jonah and the fish. Then, glue the picture to a piece of poster board. Your teacher will help you cut out the puzzle. You can have fun putting the puzzle back together. Try to match the fish pieces. Then, take it apart and try to spell F-I-S-H. Do the puzzle again and try to spell O-B-E-Y.

Jonah

Traveling to Nineveh

Jonah 3:1-3

Memory Verse

He is faithful...to forgive us.
I John 1:9

For the Teacher

Duplicate this page and the Jonah pattern on page 36 for each child. NOTE: The Jonah pattern is also used with the Prayer Box on page 36. Let the children color and cut out Jonah. Help them glue Jonah to a spring-type clothespin, using the two ends as feet. Discuss the story of Jonah. Explain that we make mistakes but God understands. He gives us a chance to start over again, just like Jonah.

Introduction

God told Jonah to go to Nineveh. Jonah decided to go to a different city instead. While traveling there by boat, Jonah was tossed into the sea during a terrible storm. A giant fish swallowed him. After the fish spit Jonah out on the beach, Jonah followed God's directions and traveled to Nineveh. He told the people an important message from God.

The Road to Nineveh

You can help Jonah get to Nineveh. First, make a toy figure of Jonah. Color him and cut him out. Glue him on a clothespin. While this dries, trace the different roads on the picture with your finger. Try to find the road that is not broken. When you find the path that goes to Nineveh without breaking, use the figure of Jonah to walk along that road.

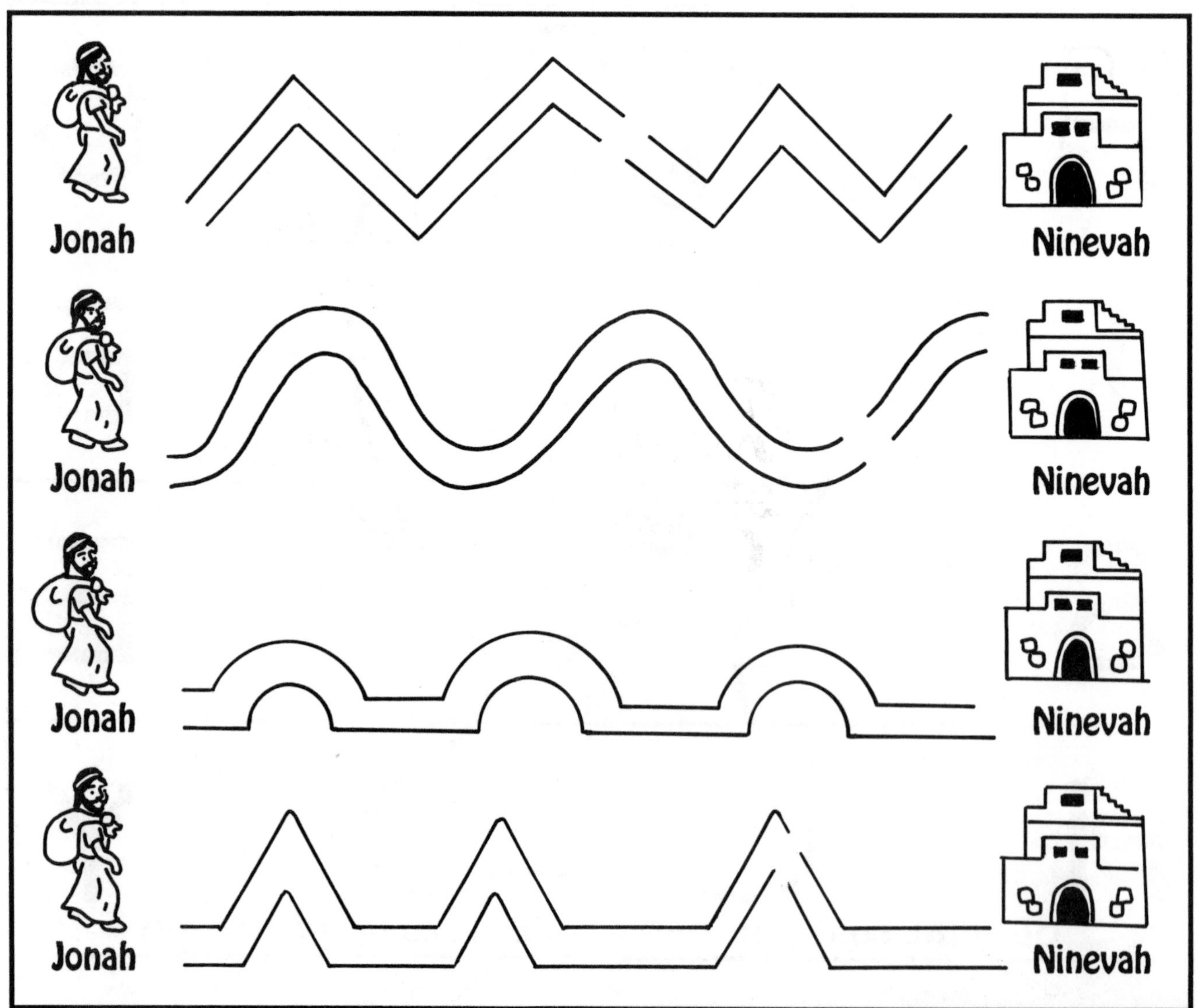

Jonah

Preaching God's Message

Jonah 3:4-10

Memory Verse

O my God; Your law is within my heart.
Psalm 40:8

For the Teacher

Duplicate a pattern page for each child. Use the large circle to cut the following for each child: one red circle, one yellow circle, and one green circle. Help the children glue the circles on a black piece of construction paper to represent a traffic signal. Glue *STOP* in the center of the red circle, *WAIT* in the yellow circle, and *GO* in the green circle.

Introduction

When Jonah arrived in Nineveh, he told the people an important message from God. Jonah said that the city would be destroyed in forty days because everyone was doing evil things. When the king heard Jonah's announcement, he made a new law! The law told the people to stop doing wrong things. Next, it told the people to pray to God and do good things.

Stop and Go!

The people followed the new law. God saw them change their ways. God decided to allow the people to live. The king's new law had worked just like a traffic signal. Make a traffic signal to help you remember to make the right choices, too. Glue the red, yellow, and green circles on the black paper. Then, glue the messages inside the circles.

HINT: Hand younger children one circle at a time and show them where to glue it.

STOP
doing
wrong!

WAIT!
Listen
to God.

GO!
Do good
things.

Completed Signal

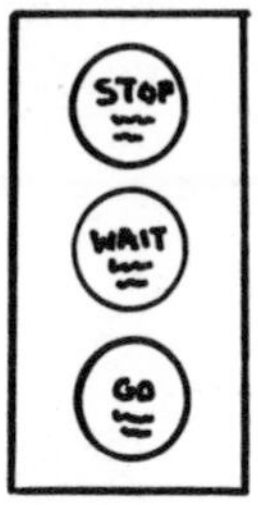

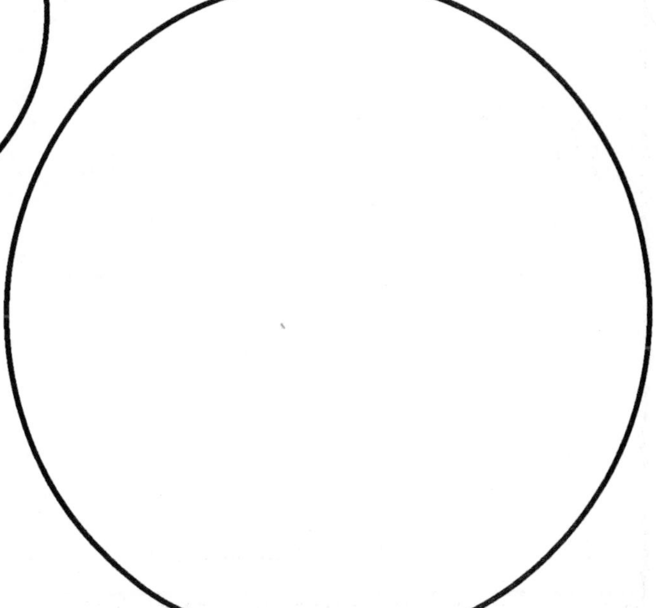

Jesus

Willing to Die for Us

John 17:20-26; Mark 2:1-12; Luke 19:1-10; 24:1-12

Memory Verse

The gift of God is eternal life.
Romans 6:23

For the Teacher

Give each child: one red felt heart the size of the heart below, one small adhesive bandage, a 1 x 3 ½-inch strip of sandpaper, a facial tissue lightly scented with perfume, and a 2 ½ x 3-inch piece of foil. Duplicate pattern pages 40, 41, and 42 for each child. Precut the book pages. After the children color the pages, hand them the items to attach to each page: the felt heart for page one, the bandage for the girl's leg on page two, sandpaper for the road on page three, and tissue for the tomb on page four. Staple the pages together and cover the staples with colored tape to prevent scratching.

Introduction

Jesus is God's Son. He traveled throughout Israel to share the Gospel. When He died on the cross and rose from the dead, He showed us that He loved us very much. Each of us can choose to believe Jesus died for us. We can become members of His family and will one day live in heaven with Him.

Resurrection Touch-It Book

Color the pages. Glue an item on each page. Smell the tissue. After you glue foil on the last page, look in the mirror. Remember, Jesus loves you!

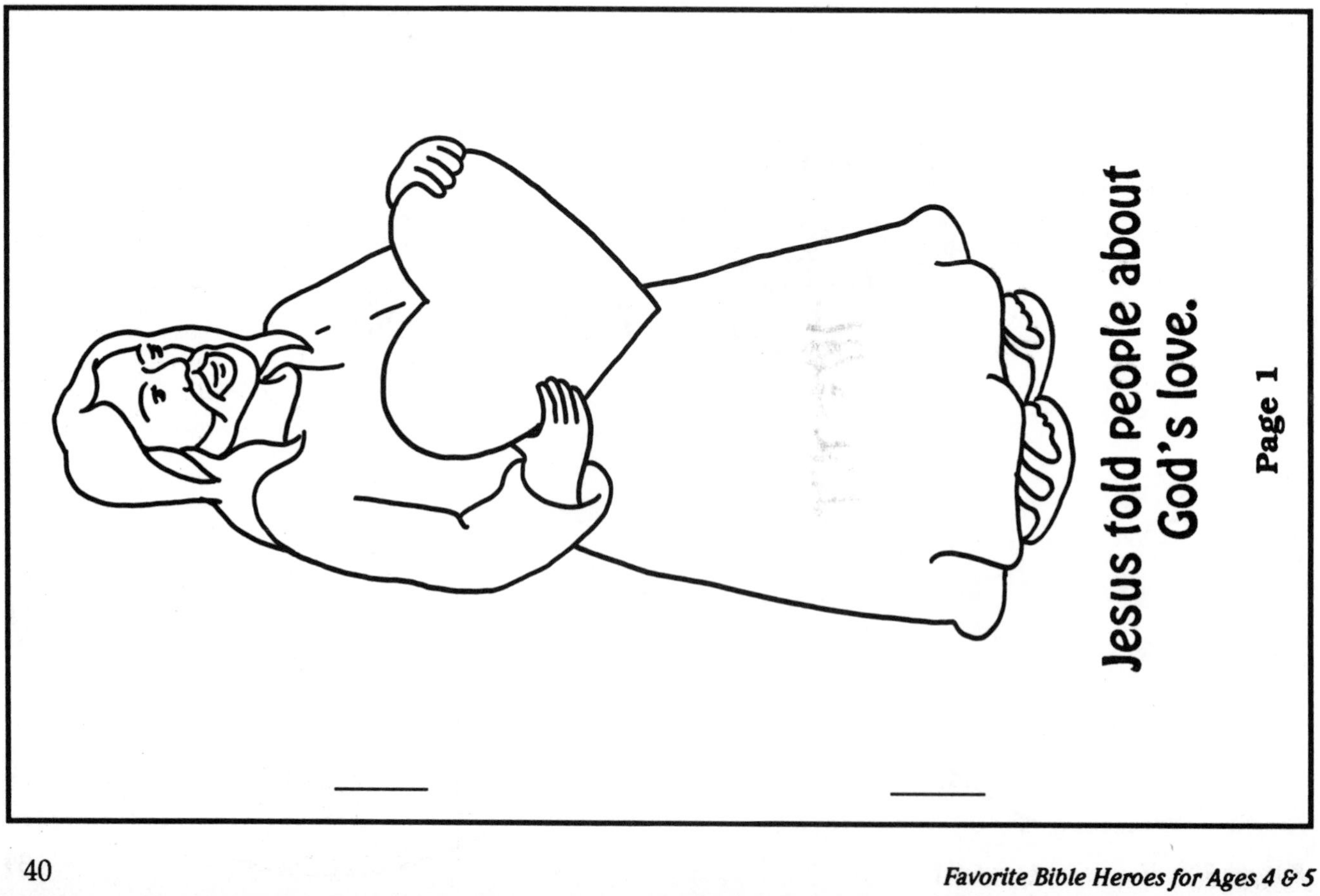

Jesus told people about God's love.

Page 1

Jesus healed people and helped them.
Page 2
Jesus walked to many places to teach the people about God.
Page 3

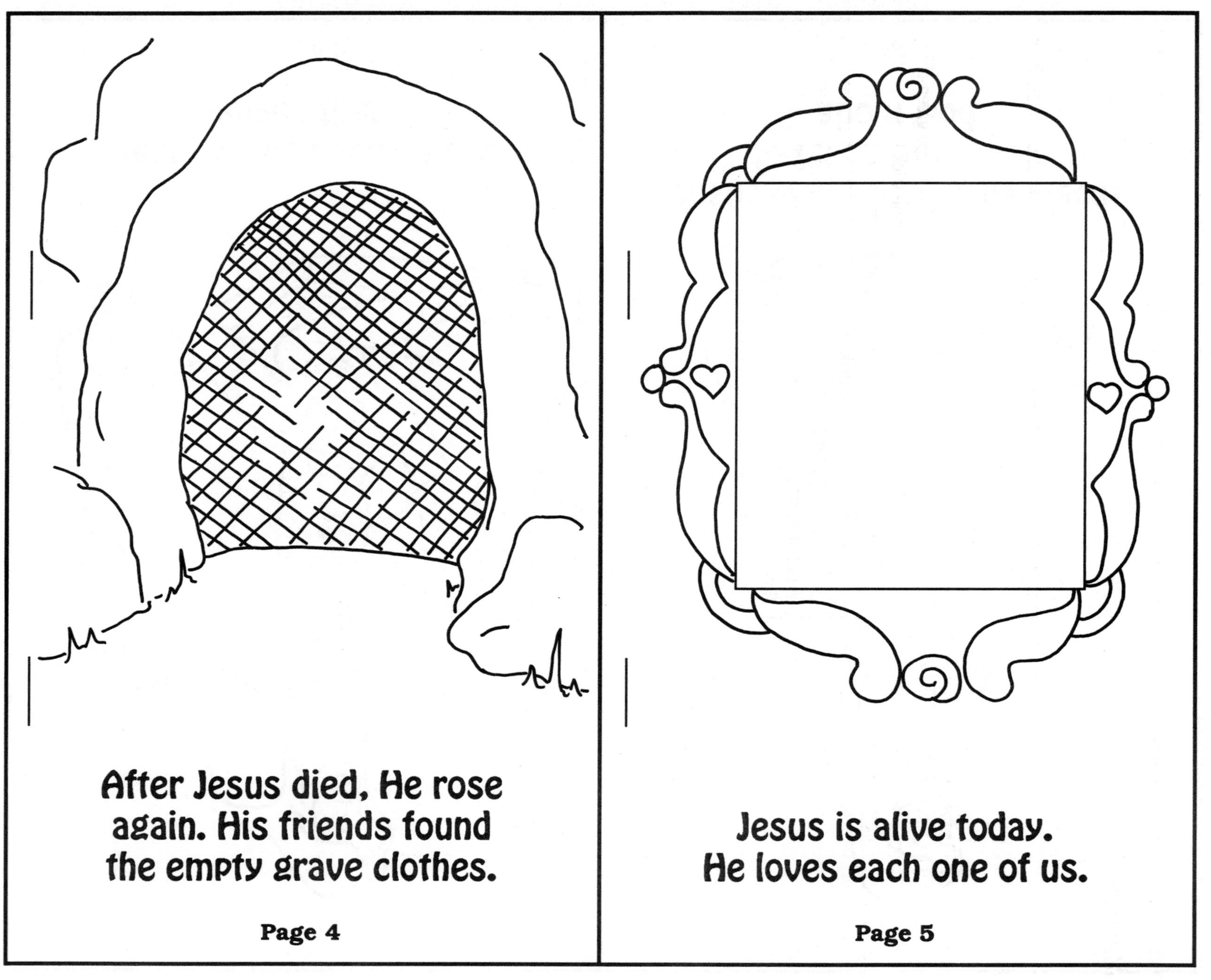
After Jesus died, He rose again. His friends found the empty grave clothes.
Page 4
Jesus is alive today. He loves each one of us.
Page 5

Jesus

God Takes Care of Us

Luke 12:22-31

Memory Verse

Do not worry.
Luke 12:22 (NIV)

For the Teacher

Duplicate this page and cut a small paper cup in half for each child. Add green tempera paint to glue. Leave the glue in the bottles for easy decorating. Before class, glue one muffin paper cup inside the other. Provide two double muffin cups, tissue paper, and a piece of poster board for each child.

Introduction

Jesus talked about lilies in this story. He told us not to worry. He reminded us that lilies are very beautiful flowers. Lilies do not worry about anything. Jesus explained that God takes care of the lilies. Jesus told us that God will take care of us, too.

The Lilies

Glue this page to a piece of poster board. Use colored green glue to decorate the stems and leaves. Next, use a glue stick to spread glue on the circles. Press paper muffin cups on the circles and decorate them with colored glue to make pretty flowers. Spread glue on the cut portion of the paper cup half. Glue the cup to the page as a flower pot. When dry, crumple tissue paper in the cup for grass. Think about the flowers and how God takes care of them. You can say, "Thank You, God, for promising that You will take care of me."

Do not worry. — Luke 12:22 (NIV)

Peter

A Fisher of Men

Mark 1:16-18

Memory Verse

"Come, follow Me," Jesus said.
Mark 1:17 (NIV)

For the Teacher

Using the fish pattern, cut six poster board fish for each child. Cut an adhesive-backed magnetic strip into ½-inch pieces, six per child. Help each child stick one strip on each fish. Demonstrate how to tape one end of an 18-inch piece of thick yarn onto the end of a plastic drinking straw. On the other end of the yarn, tie a large metal paper clip. Make a bucket from a 32-ounce yogurt, cottage cheese, or sour cream container by punching two holes opposite each other near the top edge. The children may decorate the buckets with fish stickers (or duplicate the fish patterns onto colorful paper and help them glue the fish on the buckets). Tie a 12-inch piece of thick yarn through the holes to form a handle. Show the children how to hold the pole and catch fish to put in the bucket.

Fisherman Game

Pretend you are a fisherman just like Peter. Try to catch all your fish and put them in your bucket. Peter followed Jesus. He learned how to share God's love with other people. This made Peter a fisher of men. You can be a fisher of men when you follow Jesus and tell others of God's love. Sharing your game is a fun way to start.

Introduction

Strong Simon Peter tossed his fishing net into the Sea of Galilee. His brother Andrew helped him. They were fishermen. Jesus walked beside the lake and saw what they were doing. "Come, follow Me!" called Jesus. "I will make you fishers of men!" Peter and Andrew dropped their nets. They followed Jesus and learned how to teach people about God's love.

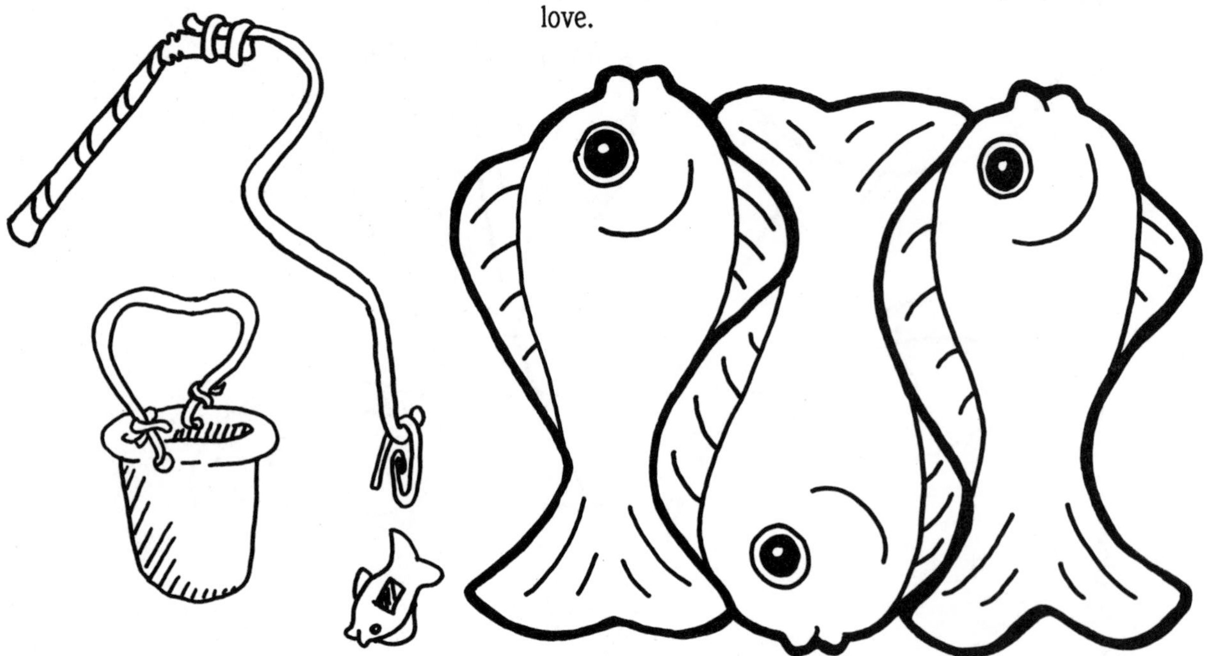

Completed Game

Peter

The Miracle of the Fish
John 21:1-14

Memory Verse
It is the Lord!
John 21:7

For the Teacher
Duplicate a pattern page for each child to color and glue onto construction paper or poster board. Place small cups of glue and cotton swabs on the table. Show the children how to paint the glue carefully on the net and the boat. Provide fish-shaped crackers to glue on the net and pretzel sticks to represent the wooden boat. Bring extra pretzels and crackers for snacking.

Introduction
After Jesus rose from the dead, He visited the disciples. One time Jesus visited them when the disciples were fishing. Peter and the others tried to fish all night, but they caught nothing. Jesus appeared on the shore and told them to throw their nets on the other side of the boat. Peter threw the net into the water. A miracle happened! The net filled up full with fish.

A Fishy Picture
Look carefully at this picture as you color it. See how Peter's net is empty? You can help him fill it up by gluing the fish crackers onto the net. Glue pretzel sticks onto the boat. When Peter saw the miracle that Jesus did with the fish, it helped him believe that Jesus was actually the Son of God. When we read this story in the Bible, it helps us know that Jesus is special because He is God's Son.

HINT: Instead of using fish crackers, cut fish shapes from colorful paper or poster board. The children can use a glue stick to attach the paper fish to the net.

Peter

Feed My Sheep

John 21:12-19

Memory Verse

Jesus said, "Feed My sheep."
John 21:17 (NIV)

For the Teacher

Make several sugar cookies for each child. Make extras for the children to eat. Provide a lunch-size paper sack and a recipe card for each child. Draw the outline of a sheep on each sack. Mix 2 egg yolks with ½ teaspoon water, divide the mixture into 6 muffin tins or custard cups, and add a few drops of food coloring to each dish. Use new brushes to paint the cookies. Each child may glue cotton balls on a paper sack to create a fluffy sheep.

Introduction

One day after His resurrection, Jesus visited the disciples. He cooked breakfast for them. Jesus then asked Simon Peter, "Simon son of John, do you truly love Me?" Peter assured Jesus that he did. Jesus asked this question three times. Each time, Peter told Jesus of his love. Each time, Jesus then asked Peter to feed His sheep.

Cookies to Share

When Jesus asked Peter to feed His sheep, Jesus was really asking Peter to tell other people about God's love. As you decorate cookies today, think of someone you can give them to as a present. If this person is a neighbor or a friend, maybe you could invite him to come to church with you. By doing this, you are helping Peter tell others about God. Glue cotton balls on a paper sack to make a fluffy sheep. Cut out a recipe card and place it in the bag with the cookies.

Completed Cookie Bag

Sugar Cookies

½ cup butter	1 teaspoon milk
¾ cup sugar	1 ¼ cups flour
1 egg	⅛ teaspoon salt
½ teaspoon vanilla	¼ teaspoon baking powder

Preheat the oven to 350°. Cream the butter. Gradually add sugar, beating until light. Add egg, vanilla, and milk. Beat thoroughly. Mix the flour, salt, and baking powder. Add to the first mixture and blend well. Arrange by spoonfuls on cookie sheets, one inch apart. Bake 8-10 minutes or until browned.

Peter

Jesus Makes a Difference

Acts 3:1-10

Memory Verse

In the name of Jesus Christ... walk.
Acts 3:6

For the Teacher

Duplicate a pattern page for each child. Encourage each child to locate the five differences by herself and color them. Talk about the positive impact Jesus can have on each person's life. Share examples of how Jesus can comfort us when we are afraid and help us make the right choice in a difficult situation.

Introduction

Peter and John walked towards the temple. A man saw them. This man had never been able to walk. He asked the disciples for money. Peter looked at the man and said, "I don't have silver or gold, but I will give you something. In the name of Jesus, walk." Peter took the man's hand and the man stood up and walked. Everyone was happy and rejoiced. They knew that they had seen another miracle.

What's the Difference?

In this story, we learn that Jesus makes a difference in people's lives. Jesus healed the man's legs when Peter prayed for him. Look at the two pictures below. There are things that are different in the two pictures. Can you find them? Color in the differences when you find them. Think about how Jesus can make a difference in your own life.

In the name of Jesus Christ . . . walk. — Acts 3:6

Philip

Jesus Feeds Five Thousand People

John 6:5-13

Memory Verse

Jesus said... "I am the bread of life."
John 6:35

For the Teacher

Duplicate a basket pattern for each child. Prior to class, cut out the baskets and many ⅛ x 3-inch strips of construction paper. Give each child an individually wrapped package of crackers and a paper on which a classmate's name is written. Explain that each child should put his crackers in that classmate's basket. Say the classmate's name as you hand each child a slip of paper.

Introduction

When Jesus saw a large crowd, He asked Philip where enough bread could be bought to feed everyone. Philip answered that eight months' wages wouldn't buy enough bread! Jesus next used a boy's five loaves and two fish to feed the five thousand men. Because this boy shared his lunch, Jesus performed a miracle that taught Philip and the disciples a lesson.

Sharing Bread Basket

Glue the basket to a piece of construction paper to form a pocket. Next, glue different colored strips of paper on the basket for decoration. Now you are ready to play a sharing game. Your teacher will give you some crackers and explain how to play the game. While you put your crackers in your classmate's basket, try to think of other ways you can share.

Completed Basket

Philip

Praying in the Upper Room

Acts 1:12-14

Memory Verse

They all joined together...in prayer.
Acts 1:14 (NIV)

For the Teacher

Duplicate a picture for each child. Provide tiny stickers for the children to place on the three matching people. Discuss the importance of prayer. Explain that prayer is talking to God. Encourage the children to pray when they are happy and when they are sad and need help. Follow Philip's example of praying with the believers by praying together as a group.

Introduction

After Jesus died and rose again, Philip met with the other followers in an upper room. Philip and the others could have run away from God during the lonely and difficult times after Jesus' death. Instead, they met together and prayed. We can follow their example today. We can pray to ask God for help during a difficult time.

Upper Room Match

Look at this picture. There are three people that match in this picture. Can you find all three and put a sticker on them? This is a picture of Philip and the followers of Jesus as they prayed together in the upper room. It was a lonely time for Philip and his friends. They felt sad and missed Jesus. Praying and talking to God helped them feel joyful again.

They all joined together . . . in prayer. — Acts 1:14 (NIV)

Philip

Sharing the Good News

Acts 8:26-40

Memory Verse

Philip...told him the Good News about Jesus.
Acts 8:35 (NIV)

For the Teacher

Duplicate pattern pages 50 and 51 for each child. For each child, fold an 11 x 17-inch piece of construction paper in half and cut out handles as shown. For the inside of each kit provide a pocket package of facial tissues, a 3-inch square of waxed paper, a large envelope, two cheerful greeting cards, four stickers, and two adhesive bandages. Help the children glue the items inside the kit. Say the rhyme together several times. Say, **You can give a facial tissue to someone who is crying. If someone hurts herself, offer her a bandage. Share a sticker or a card with someone who is lonely.**

Introduction

An angel sent Philip on a wonderful mission. He sent Philip to meet an Ethiopian who sat in his chariot studying scripture. Philip shared the good news about Jesus with the Ethiopian. The man from Ethiopia became a believer. Children can follow Philip's example and share the gospel, too. By doing kind acts for others, we can demonstrate Jesus' love.

Good News Kit

You can make a special kit to share Jesus' love with your friends and family. Color and glue the poem on the front of the kit. Print your name at the bottom. On the inside, glue a package of facial tissues, a 3-inch square of waxed paper, and a large envelope. Glue the memory verse on the large envelope and put two cheerful cards inside. Glue the bandage picture to form a pocket. Put two adhesive bandages in the pocket. Place four stickers on the waxed paper. Think about how each item can be used to help a friend. When you use your kit, say the rhyme on the front to tell the person about Jesus' love.

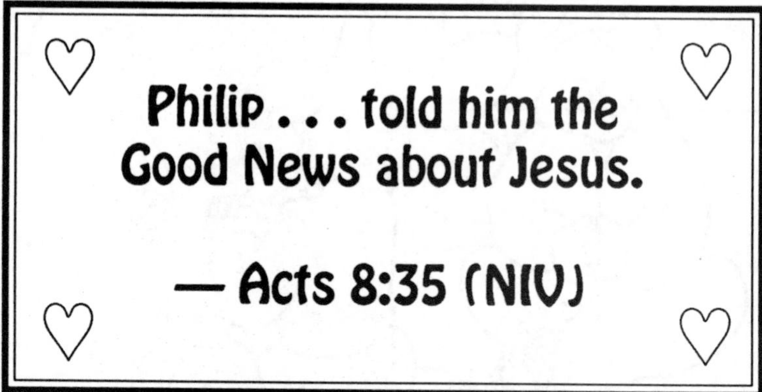

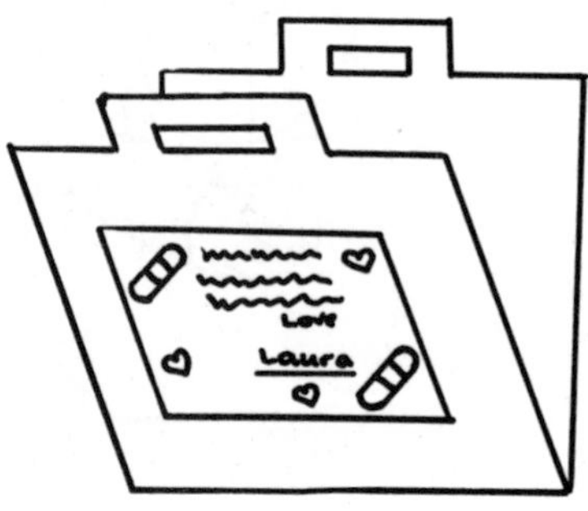

Completed Kit

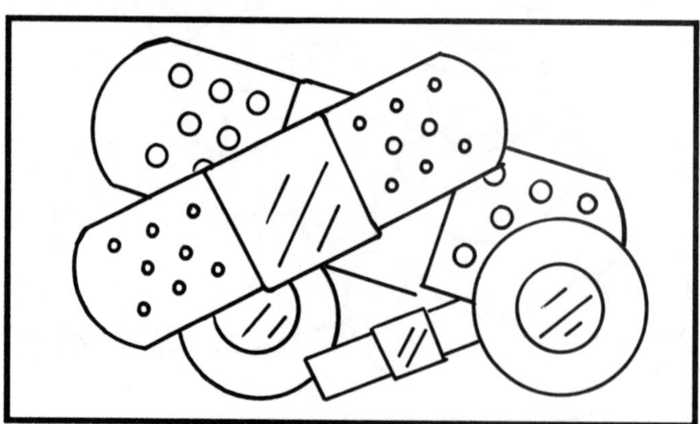

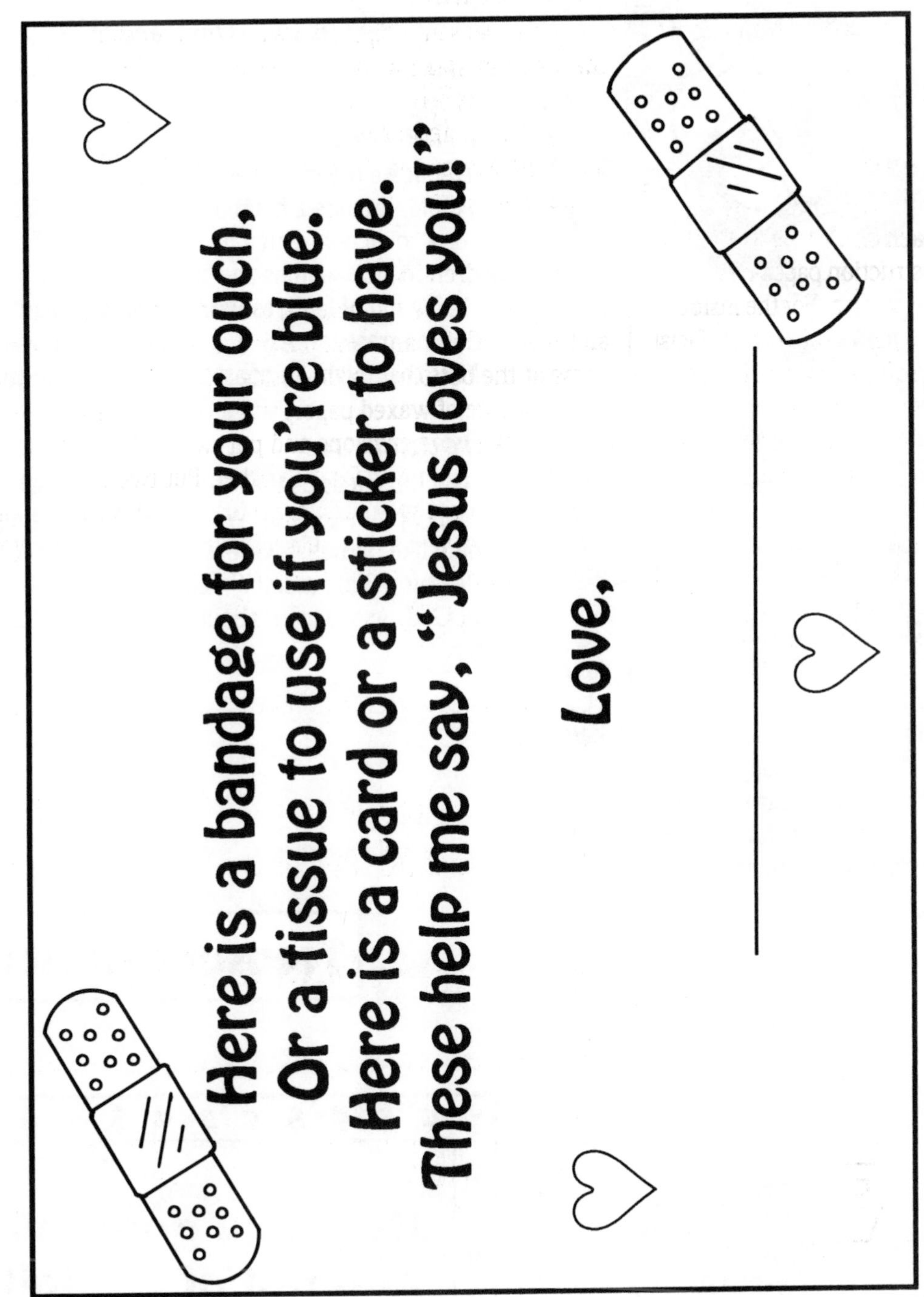
Here is a bandage for your ouch,
Or a tissue to use if you're blue.
Here is a card or a sticker to have.
These help me say, "Jesus loves you!"
Love,

Barnabas

A Good Man, Full of Faith

Acts 11:19-30

Memory Verse

He was a good man, and full of...faith.
Acts 11:24

For the Teacher

Duplicate the memory verse and chest label patterns for each child. Provide a hamburger box from a fast-food restaurant or a small box with a lid for each child. Encourage the children to glue sequins and stickers on their boxes. Explain that being full of faith, as Barnabas was, is an eternal and everlasting treasure. Ask the children to describe other godly qualities that might be considered as valuable treasures.

Introduction

The Bible tells us that Barnabas was a godly man, full of the Holy Spirit and faith. We can ask God to help us grow to become like Barnabas. One way to start is by reading the Bible and learning Bible memory verses. God's Word helps us learn about God. As we learn about God, He helps us more and more.

Faith Treasure Chest

Make a Treasure Box in which to keep your memory verses and other important objects. Decorate the box with sequins, pieces of foil, and stickers to make it shiny. Then put a copy of your memory verse inside. Each time you learn a new verse, you can ask an adult to write it down. Add the new memory verse to your treasure box.

Treasure Chest

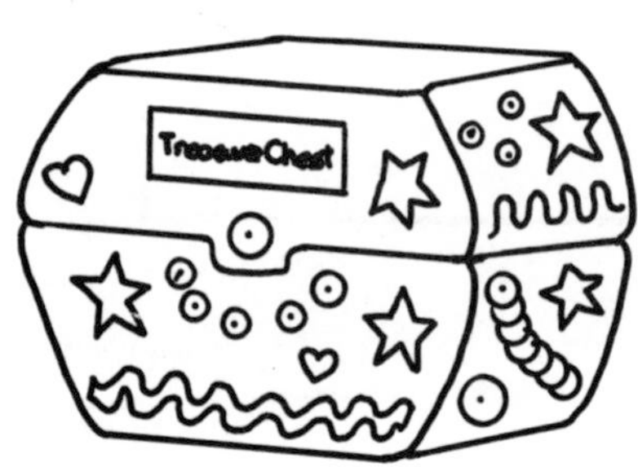

Completed Chest

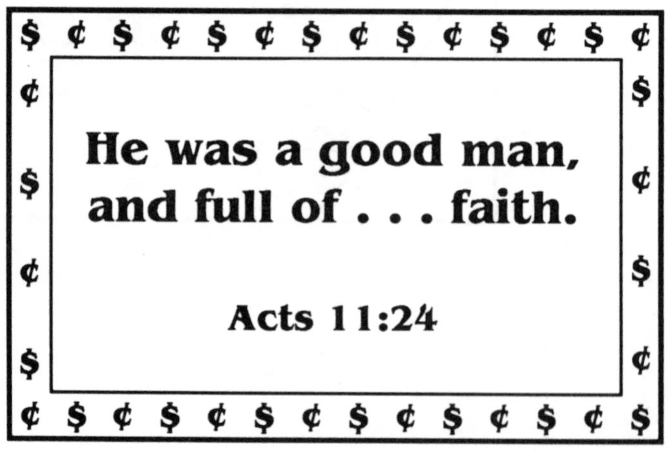

Barnabas

Overcome Fears

Acts 9:26-30

Memory Verse

I will trust, and not be afraid.
Isaiah 12:2

For the Teacher

Duplicate a flag pattern onto bright paper for each child and cut it out. Provide fluorescent paint, markers, or rubber stamps. Help the children decorate their flags. Glue the flags at the top of 14-inch long dowel rods. Use clear tape to reinforce the glued edge. Play some lively marching music. Enthusiastically recite the memory verse while everyone marches around the room.

Introduction

After Saul was converted on the road to Damascus, many of the believers did not think he actually dedicated his life to Jesus. Many were afraid that this was a plot of Saul's to capture them as prisoners. But Barnabas, a brave man of God, brought Saul to the believers and explained that Saul was really a new disciple.

Flag of Bravery

Sometimes we feel scared. The darkness seems frightening to us or we worry about a noise in the night. We can make a flag to keep in our room to remind us to trust in God whenever we feel afraid. We can be brave like Barnabas was because we know God loves us. God will help us not to be afraid anymore. Decorate your flag and tape it to a dowel rod. Then, have a parade around the room.

HINT: If dowel rods are not available, join three plastic drinking straws together. Do not use flexible straws. On two straws, cut a 1/2-inch slit at one end. Slide the slit ends inside the other ends of the straws. Secure with clear plastic tape.

I will trust,
and not be afraid.
— Isaiah 12:2

Completed Flag

Barnabas

Telling People About Jesus

Acts 11:19-30

Memory Verse

People were brought to the Lord.
Acts 11:24 (NIV)

For the Teacher

Duplicate a set of puppets for each child. Spread glue on the back of the puppets and glue them to poster board. When dry, cut them out. Use a hole punch to help cut out the finger holes. After the children color the puppets, help them glue fabric for clothes. Tell a story about Barnabas sharing the gospel. Encourage the children to move their puppets as you tell the story.

Introduction

Barnabas told many people about Jesus. He traveled often with Paul, teaching the Good News everywhere. Through his teachings and his godly example, many people came to know Jesus as their personal Savior. While using these finger puppets, the children can practice telling another person about Jesus.

Witnessing Finger Puppets

You can make these finger puppets to act out Barnabas' travels. Color the puppets and glue on clothes. Place one puppet on each hand by sticking two fingers through the holes. Pretend the man puppet is Barnabas. March your fingers around as if he is walking. Imagine that the other puppet is a person that Barnabas meets. Have Barnabas tell the person about Jesus. Use your fingers to pretend that the person is praying to Jesus.

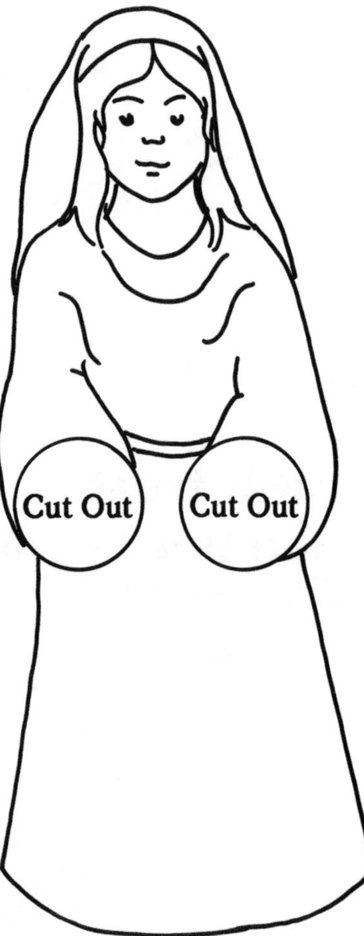

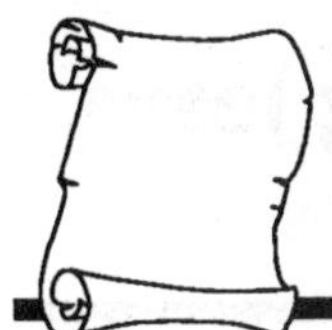

Barnabas

Teaching the Christians

Acts 11:19-30

Memory Verse

The disciples were called Christians.
Acts 11:26

For the Teacher

Duplicate a face pattern for each child. Let the children color, cut, and glue the face to look like themselves. Provide yellow, brown, black, and red yarn for hair. Take time to offer each child the opportunity to accept Jesus and become part of God's family. Be sensitive to the child who is not ready to make this decision. Pray for each child with your co-workers.

Introduction

Barnabas taught the people in Antioch [AN tih ock] about Jesus. A great number of people believed what he taught. They were first called Christians in this city. The color of their skin or the shape of their eyes did not matter. The reason they were called Christians was because they believed in Christ Jesus and accepted Him as their Savior.

The Face of a Christian

Color the face pattern to look like you. Color the skin to match yours. Color the eyes, nose, and mouth to look like your own. Glue these on the empty face. Glue yarn on the picture to look like your hair. Each person's picture will seem different because each person looks different. Yet, everyone who accepts Jesus as his Savior and Friend is a Christian.

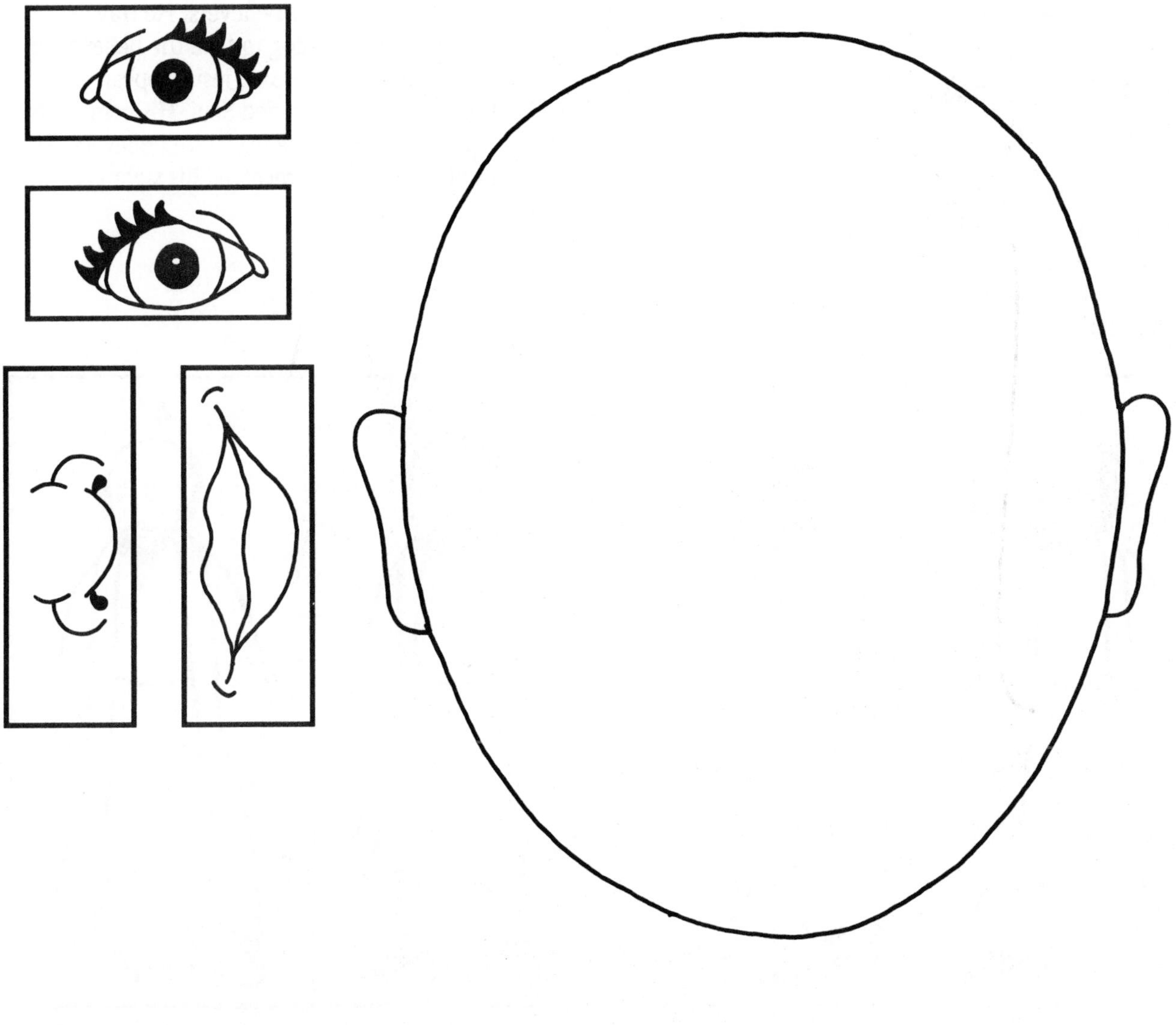

Paul

Going Blind and Meeting Jesus

Acts 9:1-9

Memory Verse

He began to preach...that Jesus is the Son of God.
Acts 9:20 (NIV)

For the Teacher

This game is played like Pin the Tail on the Donkey. Duplicate the street patterns on pages 57, 58, and 59 one time. Hang the pictures on the wall at the children's eye level to form a mural of one long street. Duplicate the pictures of Saul, one per child. Cut them apart. Apply a piece of clear tape to the back of each picture of Saul so that it will stick easily to the picture on the wall. Use a piece of fabric or a scarf as a blindfold. Explain that Saul is trying to find the door with an X on it. (You may want to color it a bright color.)

Introduction

Saul plotted to destroy the early believers. He traveled along the road to Damascus, planning to take the believers of that city as prisoners. While on the road, Jesus appeared to Saul in a brilliant light. The light blinded Saul. His companions led blind Saul to Damascus where he met with believers. Saul then dedicated his life to Jesus and received his sight again.

Take Saul to Damascus!

Put the blindfold on and allow your teacher to spin you around. No peeking! Take Saul to the house in Damascus marked with an X. Try to place him in front of the correct door without looking. Pretend you are blind like Saul. Try to imagine what it must have felt like to not be able to see. Then, take off the blindfold to see where you placed Saul.

Glue page 59 pattern here.

Glue page 57 pattern here.

Paul

Spreading God's Word

Acts 12-14

Memory Verse

The Word of God ...spread.
Acts 12:24 (NIV)

For the Teacher

Duplicate the instructions and verse boxes for each child. Cut a window from the center of each 9 x 12-inch piece of construction paper: fold the paper in half, place the rectangle on the fold, and cut around it. Open the construction paper to form a frame. For each child, provide a self-closing plastic sandwich bag, seeds, cotton balls, and paper hearts and leaves.

Introduction

Saul, whose name was changed to Paul, did many things to spread the Word of God. He traveled to different cities and told the people about Jesus. He wrote letters to various churches and explained how Jesus wanted the people to live. Every time he talked about Jesus, it was as if he planted a seed. The seeds of faith grew in people's hearts.

The Garden of Faith

Decorate the paper frame. Glue the memory verse on it. Glue hearts and leaves around the edges. Tape the instructions to the back of the frame. Pick out some seeds and drop them into the sandwich bag. Add several moist cotton balls. Your teacher will close your bag and staple it to the frame. Put tape over the staples to prevent scratching. Take your garden home and tape it to a sunny window.

Cut this window out of the center of a 9 x 12-inch sheet of construction paper.

Place on fold

The word of God . . . spread.

Acts 12:24 (NIV)

Tape me to a sunny window and watch me grow!

Completed Garden

Paul

Traveling for God

Acts 13-21

Memory Verse

He traveled,...speaking many words of encouragement.
Acts 20:2 (NIV)

For the Teacher

Duplicate pattern pages 61, 62, and 63 for each child. Tape pages 62 and 63 together. Let the children color the arrows on the map red. Cut out Paul. Provide clean plastic lids from gallon-size liquid detergent bottles, furniture polish, or deodorant cans as toy boats. Give the children cereal circles to represent Paul's words of encouragement. Bring extra cereal for snacking.

Introduction

Paul traveled wherever God sent him. Sometimes he traveled over sea by boat. Sometimes he traveled over land. Everywhere he went, he spoke words of encouragement to the people. He told them about Jesus Christ. Paul offered hope to the people as they decided to commit their lives to following Jesus.

Map It Out

Here is a map for you to color. Trace the arrows in red. Then, make a toy figure of Paul. Color the picture of Paul and glue it onto a craft stick. Put some cereal in the bottom of your toy boat. Stand Paul in the boat. Then, give Paul a ride around on the map, following the arrows from Jerusalem. Place a piece of cereal at each city. Think of ways you can encourage someone, as Paul did. Also, remember that Jesus loves you.

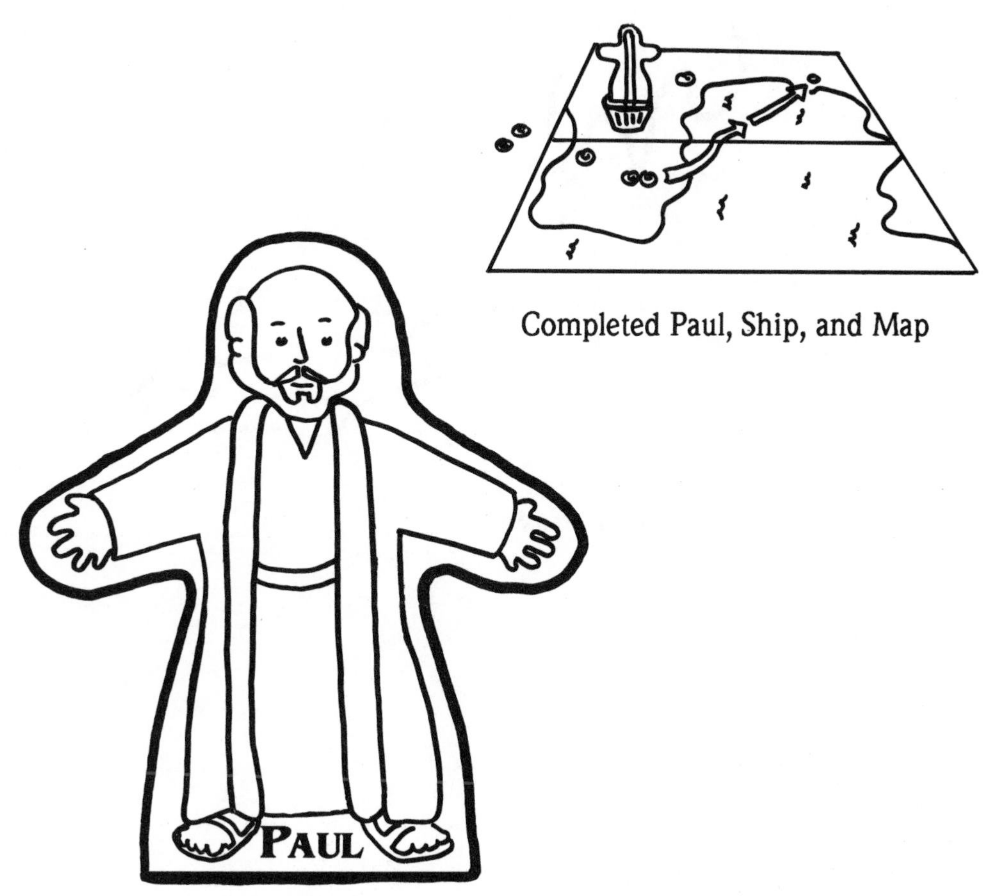

Completed Paul, Ship, and Map

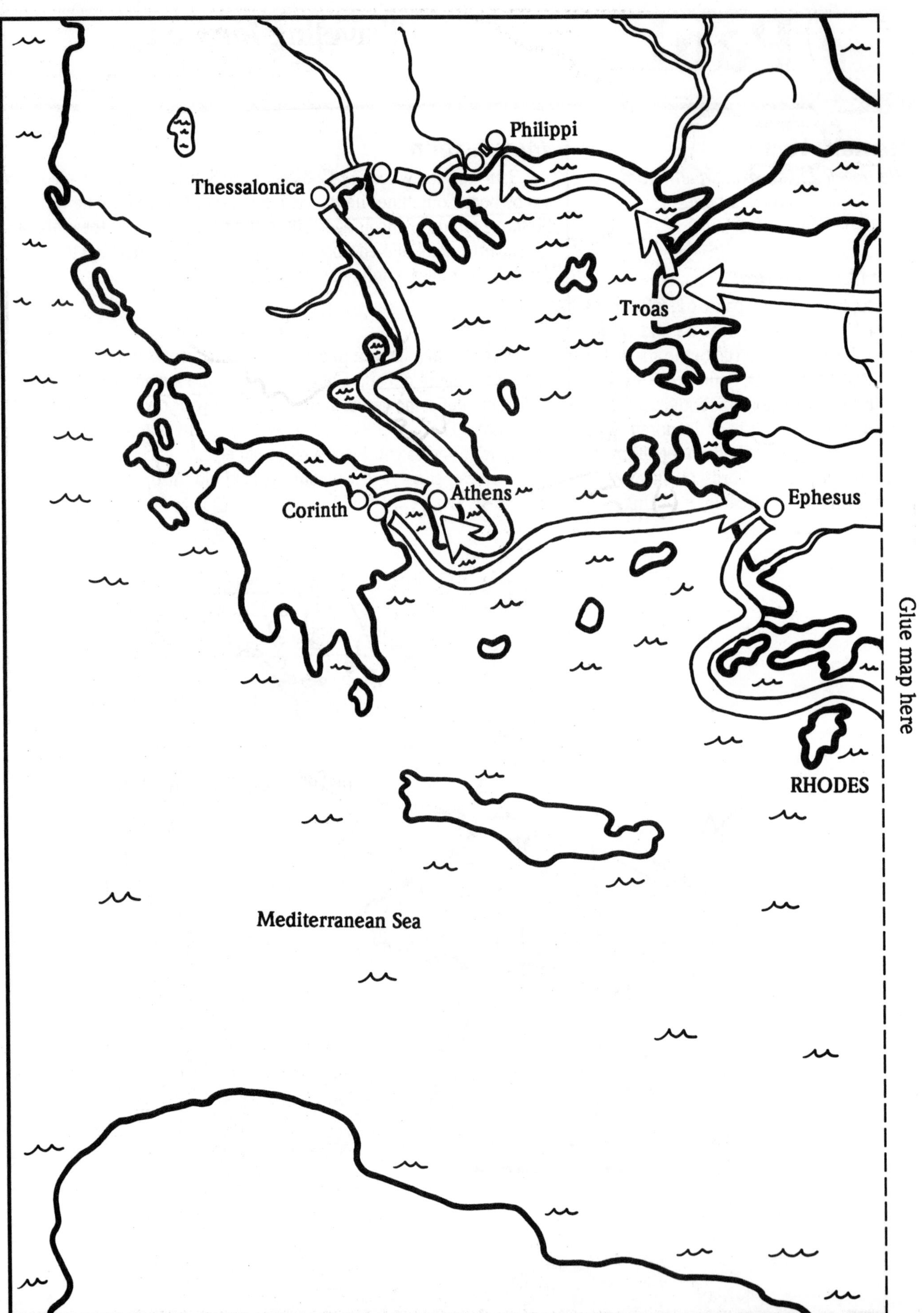
Philippi
Thessalonica
Troas
Athens
Corinth
Ephesus
RHODES
Mediterranean Sea
Glue map here

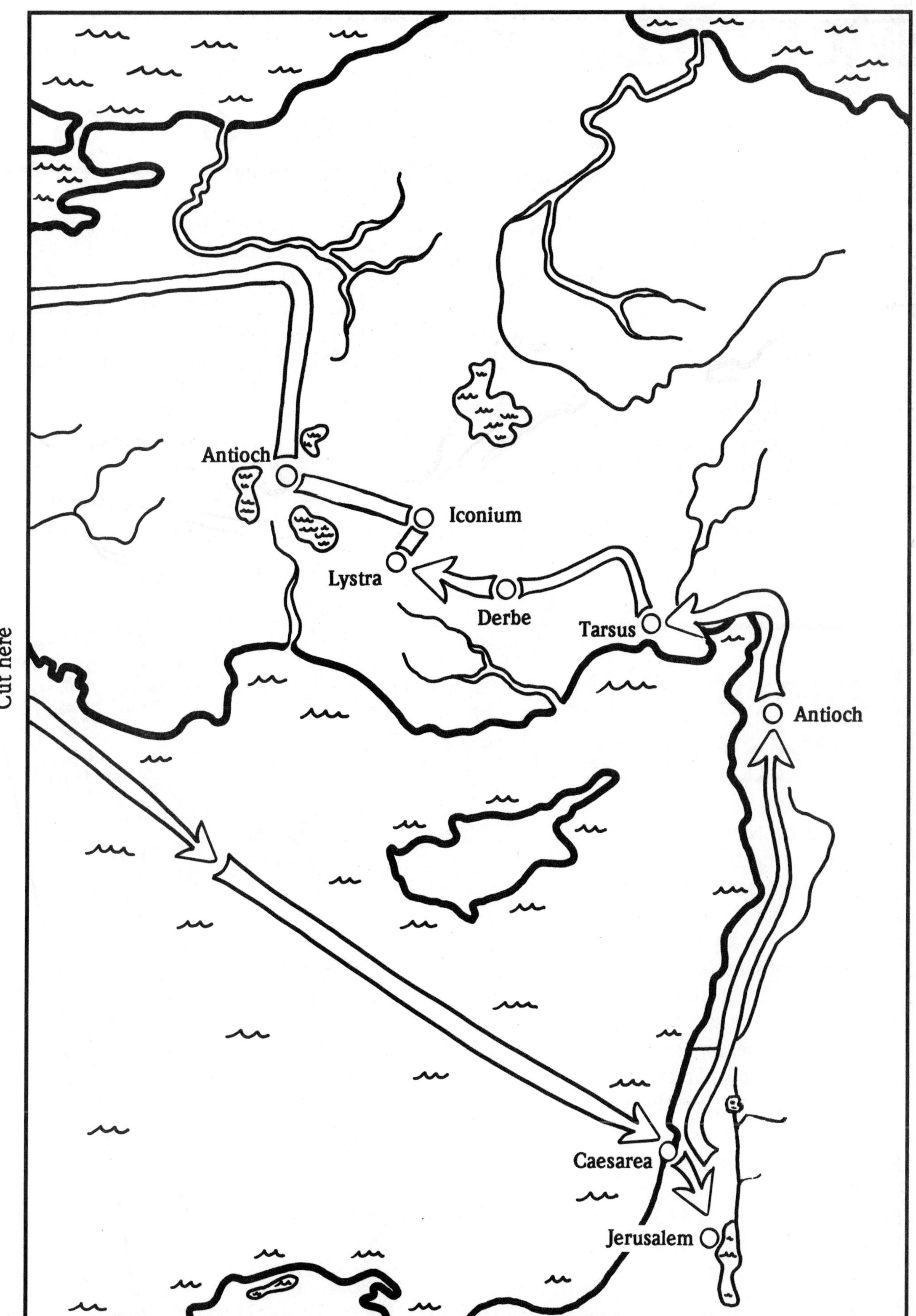
Cut here
Antioch
Iconium
Lystra
Derbe
Tarsus
Antioch
Caesarea
Jerusalem

More Bible Heroes —
Coloring PLUS Activities

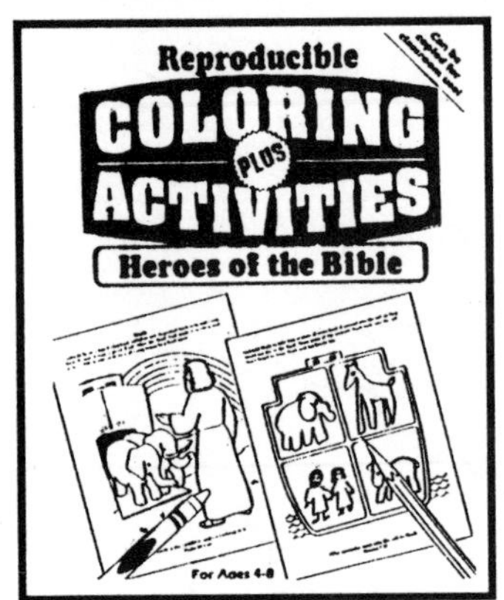

Children ages four through eight review important Bible stories and lessons and get to know additional Bible heroes with these fun-filled coloring and activity sheets.

Each coloring sheet includes a picture to color and a memory verse to reinforce lessons about Bible heroes. A related activity sheet on the other side of the page may feature a maze, dot-to-dot activity, picture to draw, hidden picture puzzle, or another hands-on Bible-teaching project.

Heroes of the Bible contains 24 coloring sheets and 24 activity sheets in these categories: Old Testament, New Testament, Bible Women, and Bible Boys and Girls. Helpful teaching tips precede each chapter with practical, easy-to-follow ideas for using the sheets to teach God's Word.

Coloring PLUS Activities: Heroes of the Bible RB37163

Favorite Bible Stories —
Teaching Activities

Old and New Testament Bible stories are creatively presented in this exciting series. Age-appropriate activities teach the Bible with cutting, coloring, pasting, puppets, puzzles, stand-up figures, crafts, mazes, and much more.

Teachers will appreciate the helpful tips provided on each activity page, the perforated pages for easy removal, and the large number of reproducible patterns included in each book.

Favorite Bible Stories Activities — Ages 2 & 3 ....RB36241
Favorite Bible Stories Activities — Ages 4 & 5 ....RB36242
Favorite Bible Stories Activities — Grades 1 & 2 ....RB36243
Favorite Bible Stories Activities — Grades 3 & 4 ....RB36244

Order from your Christian Bookstore
Rainbow Books • P. O. Box 261129 • San Diego, CA 92196